Book of Readings
on the Eucharist

Book of Readings on the Eucharist

Revised Edition

PASTORAL LITURGY SERIES • **THREE**

BISHOPS' COMMITTEE ON THE LITURGY
UNITED STATES CONFERENCE OF CATHOLIC BISHOPS
Washington, D.C.

The *Book of Readings on the Eucharist* was first developed in 2000 as a resource by the Subcommittee on the Third Millennium of the then-National Conference of Catholic Bishops; this revised edition was developed by the Bishops' Committee on the Liturgy of the United States Conference of Catholic Bishops (USCCB). It was reviewed by the chairman for the Bishops' Committee on the Liturgy, Bishop Donald W. Trautman, and has been authorized for publication by the undersigned.

Msgr. David J. Malloy, STD
General Secretary, USCCB

Cover image: Stained-glass window detail, Cathedral of St. Mary of the Immaculate Conception, Lafayette, Indiana. Photo © Jon Denker, Commercial Architectural Photographic Services. Created by Rambusch Decorating Company and Scholer Corporation.

ISBN 978-1-57455-706-0

First Printing, February 2006
Second Printing, April 2006

Contents

FOREWORD
Mass and Eucharistic Procession for the Solemnity
of the Body and Blood of Christ
POPE JOHN PAUL II vii

CHAPTER 1
The Eucharist Builds the Church
POPE JOHN PAUL II 1

CHAPTER 2
The Holy Eucharist Unites Heaven and Earth
CARDINAL FRANCIS ARINZE 7

CHAPTER 3
Eucharist in the Church and the World
CARDINAL FRANCIS GEORGE 17

CHAPTER 4
Theology of the Eucharist
ARCHBISHOP DANIEL PILARCZYK 31

CHAPTER 5
Eucharist and Trinity
FR. J. AUGUSTINE DINOIA, OP 39

CHAPTER 6
Sunday and the Eucharistic Celebration
MSGR. JAMES P. MORONEY 47

CHAPTER 7
The Eight Beatitudes of the Eucharistic Prayer
FR. CHARLES E. MILLER, CM 59

CHAPTER 8

Eucharist as Formation for Mission

Sr. Ann Rehrauer, OSF 67

CHAPTER 9

Eucharist and Justice

Sr. Joyce Ann Zimmerman, CPPS 77

CHAPTER 10

Adoration of the Blessed Sacrament

Fr. Jeremy Driscoll, OSB 85

CHAPTER 11

The Eucharist and Inculturation

Sr. Doris Mary Turek, SSND 93

FOREWORD

Mass and Eucharistic Procession for the Solemnity of the Body and Blood of Christ

Pope John Paul II

Homily at the Basilica of St. John Lateran, Thursday, June 10, 2004

1. *"As often as you eat this bread and drink this cup, you proclaim the Lord's death until he comes"* (1 Cor 11:26).

With these words St. Paul reminds the Christians of Corinth that the "Lord's Supper" is not only a convivial meeting but also, and above all, the memorial of the redeeming sacrifice of Christ. Those who take part in it, the Apostle explains, are united with the mystery of the death of the Lord, and indeed, "proclaim" him.

Thus, there is a very close relationship between *"building the Eucharist"* and *proclaiming Christ.* At the same time, entering into communion with him in the memorial of Easter also means becoming missionaries of the event which that rite actualizes; in a certain sense, it means *making it contemporary* with every epoch, until the Lord comes again.

2. Dear brothers and sisters, we are reliving this wonderful reality in today's Solemnity of *Corpus Christi,* during which the Church does not only *celebrate the Eucharist* but solemnly bears it in procession, *publicly proclaiming* that the Sacrifice of Christ is for the salvation of the whole world.

Grateful for this immense gift, her members gather round the Blessed Sacrament, for that is the source and summit of her being and action. *Ecclesia de Eucharistia vivit!* The Church draws her life from the Eucharist and knows that this truth does not simply express a daily experience of

John Paul II, Homily at the Mass and Eucharistic Procession for the Solemnity of the Body and Blood of Christ, Basilica of St. John Lateran (June 10, 2004), http://www.vatican.va/holy_father/john_paul_ii/homilies/2004/documents/hf_jp-ii_hom_20040610_corpus-domini_en.html.

faith, but recapitulates the heart of the mystery in which she consists (cf. Encyclical Letter *Ecclesia de Eucaristia*, no. 1).

3. Ever since Pentecost, when the Church, the People of the New Covenant, "began her pilgrim journey towards her heavenly homeland, the Divine Sacrament has continued to mark the passing of her days, filling them with confident hope" (ibid.). Thinking precisely of this, I wanted to dedicate the first Encyclical of the new millennium to the Eucharist and I am now pleased to announce a special *Year of the Eucharist*. It will begin with the World Eucharistic Congress, planned to take place from 10 to 17 October 2004 in Guadalajara, Mexico, and will end with the next Ordinary Assembly of the Synod of Bishops, that will be held in the Vatican from 2 to 29 October 2005 and whose theme will be: "*The Eucharist: source and summit of the life and mission of the Church*."

Through the Eucharist, the Ecclesial Community is built up as a new Jerusalem, a principle of unity in Christ among different persons and peoples.

4. "*You give them something to eat*" (Lk 9:13).

The Gospel passage we have just heard offers us a vivid image of the close bond that exists between the Eucharist and this universal mission of the Church. Christ, "the living bread which came down from heaven" (Jn 6:51; cf. *Gospel Acclamation*), is the *only one* who can appease the hunger of human beings of every time and in every corner of the earth.

However, he *does not want to do this on his own*, so he involves the disciples, as he did in the multiplication of the loaves: "*Taking the five loaves and the two fish he looked up to heaven, and blessed and broke them, and gave them to the disciples to set before the crowd*" (Lk 9:16). This miraculous sign is the symbol of the greatest mystery of love which is renewed every day at Holy Mass: through the ordained ministers, Christ gives his Body and his Blood for the life of humanity. And all those who partake of his Banquet with dignity become living instruments of his presence of love, mercy and peace.

5. "*Lauda, Sion, Salvatorem!* . . .—*Sion, praise the Saviour / your guide, your pastor / with hymns and canticles*."

With untold emotion, we hear this invitation to praise and joy echoing in our hearts. At the end of Holy Mass we will carry the Divine Sacrament in procession to the Basilica of St. Mary Major. Looking at Mary, we will understand better the transforming power that the Eucharist possesses. Listening to her, we will find in the Eucharistic mystery the courage and energy to follow Christ, the Good Shepherd, and to serve him in the brethren.

CHAPTER 1

The Eucharist Builds the Church

POPE JOHN PAUL II

Chapter 2 from Encyclical On the Eucharist (Ecclesiae de Eucharistia)

21. The Second Vatican Council teaches that the celebration of the Eucharist is at the center of the process of the Church's growth. After stating that "the Church, as the Kingdom of Christ already present in mystery, grows visibly in the world through the power of God,"[35] then, as if in answer to the question: "How does the Church grow?", the Council adds: "as often as the sacrifice of the Cross by which 'Christ our pasch is sacrificed' (1 Cor 5:7) is celebrated on the altar, the work of our redemption is carried out. At the same time in the sacrament of the Eucharistic bread, the unity of the faithful, who form one body in Christ (cf. 1 Cor 10:17), is both expressed and brought about."[36]

A *causal influence of the Eucharist* is present at the Church's very origins. The Evangelists specify that it was the Twelve, the Apostles, who gathered with Jesus at the Last Supper (cf. Mt 26:20; Mk 14:17; Lk 22:14). This is a detail of notable importance, for the Apostles "were both the seeds of the new Israel and the beginning of the sacred hierarchy."[37] By offering them his body and his blood as food, Christ mysteriously involved them in the sacrifice which would be completed later on Calvary. By analogy with the Covenant of Mount Sinai, sealed by sacrifice and the sprinkling of blood,[38] the actions and words of Jesus at the Last Supper laid the foundations of the new messianic community, the People of the New Covenant.

The Apostles, by accepting in the Upper Room Jesus' invitation: "Take, eat," "Drink of it, all of you" (Mt 26:26-27), entered for the first

---

John Paul II, "The Eucharist Builds the Church," Chapter 2 in *On the Eucharist* (*Ecclesiae de Eucharistia*) (Washington, DC: Libreria Editrice Vaticana–United States Conference of Catholic Bishops, 2003).

time into sacramental communion with him. From that time forward, until the end of the age, the Church is built up through sacramental communion with the Son of God who was sacrificed for our sake: "Do this is remembrance of me . . . Do this, as often as you drink it, in remembrance of me" (1 Cor 11:24-25; cf. Lk 22:19).

22. Incorporation into Christ, which is brought about by Baptism, is constantly renewed and consolidated by sharing in the Eucharistic Sacrifice, especially by that full sharing which takes place in sacramental communion. We can say not only that *each of us receives Christ*, but also that *Christ receives each of us*. He enters into friendship with us: "You are my friends" (Jn 15:14). Indeed, it is because of him that we have life: "He who eats me will live because of me" (Jn 6:57). Eucharistic communion brings about in a sublime way the mutual "abiding" of Christ and each of his followers: "Abide in me, and I in you" (Jn 15:4).

By its union with Christ, the People of the New Covenant, far from closing in upon itself, becomes a "sacrament" for humanity,[39] a sign and instrument of the salvation achieved by Christ, the light of the world and the salt of the earth (cf. Mt 5:13-16), for the redemption of all.[40] The Church's mission stands in continuity with the mission of Christ: "As the Father has sent me, even so I send you" (Jn 20:21). From the perpetuation of the sacrifice of the Cross and her communion with the body and blood of Christ in the Eucharist, the Church draws the spiritual power needed to carry out her mission. The Eucharist thus appears as both *the source* and *the summit* of all evangelization, since its goal is the communion of mankind with Christ and in him with the Father and the Holy Spirit.[41]

23. Eucharistic communion also confirms the Church in her unity as the body of Christ. St. Paul refers to this *unifying power* of participation in the banquet of the Eucharist when he writes to the Corinthians: "The bread which we break, is it not a communion in the body of Christ? Because there is one bread, we who are many are one body, for we all partake of the one bread" (1 Cor 10:16-17). St. John Chrysostom's commentary on these words is profound and perceptive: "For what is the bread? It is the body of Christ. And what do those who receive it become? The Body of Christ—not many bodies but one body. For as bread is completely one, though made of up many grains of wheat, and these, albeit unseen, remain nonetheless present, in such a way that their difference is not apparent since they have been made a perfect whole, so too are we

mutually joined to one another and together united with Christ."[42] The argument is compelling: our union with Christ, which is a gift and grace for each of us, makes it possible for us, in him, to share in the unity of his body which is the Church. The Eucharist reinforces the incorporation into Christ which took place in Baptism though the gift of the Spirit (cf. 1 Cor 12:13, 27).

The joint and inseparable activity of the Son and of the Holy Spirit, which is at the origin of the Church, of her consolidation and her continued life, is at work in the Eucharist. This was clearly evident to the author of the *Liturgy of St. James:* in the epiclesis of the Anaphora, God the Father is asked to send the Holy Spirit upon the faithful and upon the offerings, so that the body and blood of Christ "may be a help to all those who partake of it . . . for the sanctification of their souls and bodies."[43] The Church is fortified by the divine Paraclete through the sanctification of the faithful in the Eucharist.

24. The gift of Christ and his Spirit which we receive in Eucharistic communion superabundantly fulfils the yearning for fraternal unity deeply rooted in the human heart; at the same time it elevates the experience of fraternity already present in our common sharing at the same Eucharistic table to a degree which far surpasses that of the simple human experience of sharing a meal. Through her communion with the body of Christ the Church comes to be ever more profoundly "in Christ in the nature of a sacrament, that is, a sign and instrument of intimate unity with God and of the unity of the whole human race."[44]

The seeds of disunity, which daily experience shows to be so deeply rooted in humanity as a result of sin, are countered by *the unifying power* of the body of Christ. The Eucharist, precisely by building up the Church, creates human community.

25. The *worship of the Eucharist outside of the Mass* is of inestimable value for the life of the Church. This worship is strictly linked to the celebration of the Eucharistic Sacrifice. The presence of Christ under the sacred species reserved after Mass—a presence which lasts as long as the species of bread and of wine remain[45]—derives from the celebration of the sacrifice and is directed towards communion, both sacramental and spiritual.[46] It is the responsibility of Pastors to encourage, also by their personal witness, the practice of Eucharistic adoration, and exposition of the Blessed

Sacrament in particular, as well as prayer of adoration before Christ present under the Eucharistic species.[47]

It is pleasant to spend time with him, to lie close to his breast like the Beloved Disciple (cf. Jn 13:25) and to feel the infinite love present in his heart. If in our time Christians must be distinguished above all by the "art of prayer,"[48] how can we not feel a renewed need to spend time in spiritual converse, in silent adoration, in heartfelt love before Christ present in the Most Holy Sacrament? How often, dear brother and sisters, have I experienced this, and drawn from it strength, consolation and support!

This practice, repeatedly praised and recommended by the Magisterium,[49] is supported by the example of many saints. Particularly outstanding in this regard was St. Alphonsus Liguori, who wrote: "Of all devotions, that of adoring Jesus in the Blessed Sacrament is the greatest after the sacraments, the one dearest to God and the one most helpful to us."[50] The Eucharist is a priceless treasure: by not only celebrating it but also by praying before it outside of Mass we are enabled to make contact with the very wellspring of grace. A Christian community desirous of contemplating the face of Christ in the spirit which I proposed in the Apostolic Letters *Novo Millennio Ineunte* and *Rosarium Virginis Mariae* cannot fail also to develop this aspect of Eucharistic worship, which prolongs and increases the fruits of our communion in the body and blood of the Lord.

"In the course of the day the faithful should not omit visiting the Blessed Sacrament, which in accordance with liturgical law must be reserved in churches with great reverence in a prominent place. Such visits are a sign of gratitude, an expression of love and an acknowledgment of the Lord's presence": Paul VI, Encyclical Letter *Mysterium Fidei* (3 September 1965): AAS 57 (1965), 771.

Reflection Questions

1. What is the relationship of Baptism and Eucharist? How do the dying and rising with Christ in the first sacrament relate the reception of his Body and Blood in the second? How does each sacrament effect, or bring about, our relationship with Christ?

2. How does the Sacrament of the Eucharist effect the communion of the Church? Is the Mass always seen as the source and summit of the unity of our parishes? How can the unifying power of the body of Christ be strengthened?

3. In his writings, Pope John Paul II repeatedly emphasized the importance of restoring adoration of the Holy Eucharist outside Mass. What led many individuals and parishes to abandon adoration of the Blessed Sacrament? How can such devotion be effectively reintroduced and fostered?

Notes

35. Dogmatic Constitution *Lumen Gentium*, 3.
36. Ibid.
37. Second Vatican Ecumenical Council, Decree on the Missionary Activity of the Church *Ad Gentes*, 5.
38. "Moses took the blood and threw it upon the people, and said: 'Behold the blood of the Covenant which the Lord has made with you in accordance with all these words'" (Ex 24:8).
39. Cf. Second Vatican Ecumenical Council, Dogmatic Constitution on the Church *Lumen Gentium*, 1.
40. Cf. ibid., 9.
41. Cf. Second Vatican Ecumenical Council, Decree on the Life and Ministry of Priests *Presbyterorum Ordinis* (PO), 5. The same Decree, in no. 6, says: "No Christian community can be built up which does not grow from and hinge on the celebration of the most holy Eucharist."
42. *In Epistolam I ad Corinthios Homiliae*, 24, 2: PG 61, 200; Cf. *Didache*, IX, 4: F. X. Funk, I, 22; St. Cyprian, *Ep*. LXIII, 13: PL 4, 384.
43. PO 26, 206.
44. Second Vatican Ecumenical Council, Dogmatic Constitution on the Church *Lumen Gentium*, 1.

45. Cf. Ecumenical Council of Trent, Session XIII, *Decretum de ss. Eucharistia*, Canon 4: DS 1654.
46. Cf. *Rituale Romanum: De sacra communione et de cultu mysterii eucharistici extra Missam*, 36 (no. 80).
47. Cf. ibid., 38-39 (nos. 86-90).
48. John Paul II, Apostolic Letter *Novo Millennio Ineunte* (6 January 2001), 32: AAS 93 (2001), 288.
49. "In the course of the day the faithful should not omit visiting the Blessed Sacrament, which in accordance with liturgical law must be reserved in churches with great reverence in a prominent place. Such visits are a sign of gratitude, an expression of love and an acknowledgment of the Lord's presence": Paul VI, Encyclical Letter *Mysterium Fidei* (3 September 1965): AAS 57 (1965), 771.
50. *Visite al SS. Sacramento e a Maria Santissima*, Introduction: *Opere Ascetiche*, Avellino, 2000, 295.

The Holy Eucharist Unites Heaven and Earth

CARDINAL FRANCIS ARINZE

Address at Eucharistic Congress in the Basilica of the Immaculate Conception in Washington, D.C., on September 25, 2004

1. *Event of Grace*

The mystery of the Holy Eucharist has brought us together. Our faith in sacramental celebration of the sacrifice which our beloved Savior Jesus Christ offered of himself and then enabled the Church to continue till the end of time is manifesting itself in many ways in these two days of grace.

We all thank the Council of Major Superiors of Women Religious in the United States of America for the excellent arrangements they have made for this Eucharistic Congress.

In these two days of our faith celebration and manifestation, we celebrate the Eucharistic sacrifice; we are fed with the Body and Blood of Christ, and we have ample opportunity to adore Jesus in the Blessed Sacrament. Moreover, we have read and listened to Sacred Scripture, picked up books on the Holy Eucharist, and reflected, contemplated, and prayed. We have praised God in the Liturgy of the Hours. After the concluding Mass this evening, we are going to honor our Eucharistic Lord in solemn procession.

Reflecting on the theme of this Eucharistic Congress, "Heaven Unites with Earth," we see the Holy Eucharist as the mystery of faith in which Christ is the High Priest. This sacrifice and sacrament bring creation together and offer it to God. The Apocalypse, or the Book of Revelation, as it also known, presents a striking imagery of the heavenly Liturgy and helps us appreciate how the Eucharistic celebration, as it were, looks heavenward. At the same time, the Eucharist commits us to do our part to make this world a better place in which to live. Indeed, the Eucharist unites heaven and earth and calls for our active faith response. These will now form the points for our reflection.

2. The Holy Eucharist, Mystery of Faith

The Holy Eucharist is a great mystery of our faith. Around it are centered many of the mysteries of redemption.

After original sin, God did not abandon humanity in its sad state. He promised a Savior. In the fullness of time the Eternal Father, who is rich in mercy, sent his only-begotten Son. For love of us and for our salvation the Son of God took on human nature. He did the work of our salvation by his entire life, but especially by the Paschal Mystery of his suffering, death, and Resurrection.

The night before he freely gave his life for us in the sacrifice of the Cross, Jesus at the Last Supper gave to the Church the wonderful sacrifice and sacrament of the Holy Eucharist. He turned bread and wine into his Body and Blood. He gave the Apostles power to do the same: "Do this in memory of me" (Lk 22:19). And he gave them his Body to eat and his Blood to drink. Thus, the Council of Trent (1545-1563) teaches us, Jesus wanted "to leave to His beloved spouse the Church a visible sacrifice (as the nature of man demands) by which the bloody sacrifice which he was to accomplish once for all on the cross would be re-presented, its memory perpetuated until the end of the world, and its salutary power be applied to the forgiveness of the sins we daily commit."[1]

As sacrament, the Holy Eucharist is the Body and Blood, together with the soul and divinity, of our Lord Jesus Christ and, therefore, the whole Christ, who is truly, really and substantially present.[2] We receive him in Holy Communion.

The Eucharistic celebration—this ritual sacramental celebration of the Paschal Mystery of Christ, also called the sacrifice of the Mass—is the supreme act of the public worship of the Church. It is "the fount and apex of the whole Christian life."[3] It is an action that involves the whole Church on earth, in heaven, and in purgatory. And it has Jesus Christ as its Chief Priest and Victim. Indeed, it is he who through the Eucharistic mystery links earth to heaven, as the rest of this paper will strive to show.

3. Jesus Christ, Our High Priest

If the Eucharist unites heaven and earth, it does so mainly thanks to Jesus Christ. "The word became flesh / and made his dwelling among us" (Jn 1:14). In the incarnation, heaven comes down to earth. As the Church sings in the first Christmas preface, "In the wonder of the incarnation your eternal Word has brought to the eyes of faith a new and radiant vision of your glory. In him we see our God made visible and so are caught up in love of the God we cannot see."[4]

On earth as the Incarnate Word, Jesus Christ lifts earth to heaven by himself being the victim and the priest in his redemptive sacrifice. He was already symbolized by the paschal lamb in the exodus (cf. Ex 12:21-23). John the Baptist pointed him out: "Behold, the Lamb of God, who takes away the sin of the world" (Jn 1:29). Jesus himself was later to declare that he was freely giving his life for us: "The Father loves me, because I lay down my life in order to take it up again. No one takes it from me" (Jn 10:17-18). The Apocalypse pays Christ tribute: "Worthy is the Lamb that was slain / to receive power and riches, wisdom and strength, / honor and glory and blessing" (Rv 5:12).

In the Eucharistic sacrifice, Christ offers to his beloved bride, the Church, the possibility to be associated with him in offering to the Eternal Father a perfect sacrifice of adoration for the sins of humanity and eloquent petition in the name of Christ. Since he has taken our nature, Jesus associates us with himself in this august mystery. In himself he summarizes, recapitulates, and in a sense takes with him all humanity in this supreme act of worship.

In the Eucharist as sacrament, Jesus gives us a pledge of eternal life, a ticket for heaven. We have his own guarantee: "This is the bread that comes down from heaven so that one may eat it and not die. I am the living bread that came down from heaven; whoever eats this bread will live forever; and the bread that I will give is my flesh for the life of the world" (Jn 6:50-51).

4. Cosmic Dimension of the Holy Eucharist

One dimension of the Holy Eucharist that should not escape our attention is that Jesus associates with himself not only all humanity but also all creation, and offers all to his Eternal Father in the unity of the Holy Spirit.

The Son of God became man "to gather into one the dispersed children of God" (Jn 11:52). By the Paschal Mystery of his Passion, death, and Resurrection he redeemed humanity.

But the work of redemption goes beyond human beings in its effects and involves all creation. Original sin had turned many created things against man. And man was not always honoring God with them, as he should. The whole creation has been awaiting its own redemption, "groaning in labor pains," as St. Paul puts it (Rm 8:22). "Creation awaits with eager expectation the revelation of the children of God" (Rm 8:19).

Pope John Paul II testified that, as he in his ministry as priest, bishop, and pope has celebrated the Holy Eucharist in chapels, parish churches, basilicas, lakeshores, seacoasts, public squares, and stadiums, he has experienced the Eucharist as always in some way celebrated on the altar of the world. The Eucharist embraces and permeates all creation. "The Son of God became man in order to restore all creation, in one supreme act of praise, to the One who made it from nothing. He, the Eternal High Priest who by the blood of his Cross entered the eternal sanctuary, thus gives back to the Creator and Father all creation redeemed."[5]

St. Paul told the Colossians that the Incarnate Word is "the firstborn of all creation" and "in him all the fullness was pleased to dwell, / and through him to reconcile all things to him, / making peace by the blood of his cross / [through him], whether those on earth or those in heaven" (Col 1:15, 19-20).

And the second Christmas preface in the *Roman Missal* says of Christ: "He has come to lift up all things to Himself, to restore unity to creation, and to lead mankind from exile into your [the Father's] heavenly kingdom."

Christ entrusts the celebration of this Eucharistic sacrifice, with its cosmic dimension, to his Church. At Mass, therefore, humanity, associating with it all creation, offers the supreme act of adoration, praise, and thanksgiving through Christ, with Christ, and in Christ to the Eternal Father in the unity of the Holy Spirit.

5. Apocalyptic Imagery of the Heavenly Liturgy

The Book of Revelation speaks in prophetic and apocalyptic language with the Jerusalem temple worship as background. But it also speaks of the Church beginning to spread in the world and presents Jesus Christ as the Gospel Lamb, the King of the universe, the High Priest, the Lord of history and the immaculate Victim on his throne.

In the Apocalypse, divine worship is praise of heaven begun on earth. The cult images are powerful and clearly liturgical. Examples are adoration of the immolated Lamb on his throne, hymns and canticles, acclamations of the crowds of the elect dressed in white, descent of the Church of heaven on earth, the Jerusalem of which the Lord Jesus is the temple. And the people are a priestly and royal one. The visions recall many cult elements: seven candlesticks, the long white robe of the Son of Man, the white dress of the old men and of the saints, the altar, the Amen and the exultant Alleluia.

At the same time, the Book of Revelation also describes the exasperation of the fight between hell and the faithful of Christ, between the Woman and her children and the Beast, the false prophet who would do all in his power to seduce the inhabitants of the world.

The Eucharist is linked with this heavenly liturgy and, if well celebrated and lived on earth, will inaugurate the reign of God and dismiss the Devil and his angels.

6. The Celebrants of the Heavenly Liturgy

The *Catechism of the Catholic Church* speaks of "the celebrants of the heavenly liturgy" (no. 1137). Christ crucified and risen is the Lamb "standing as though it had been slain" (no. 1137). He is the one high priest of the true sanctuary. The river of the water of life from the throne of God and of the Lamb is a symbol of the Holy Spirit.

"Recapitulated in Christ," these are the participants in the service of the praise of God, in the heavenly liturgy: "the heavenly powers, all creation (the four living beings), the servants of the Old and New Covenants (the twenty-four elders), the new People of God (the 144,000), especially the martyrs 'slain for the word of God,' and the all-holy Mother of God (the Woman), the Bride of the Lamb, and finally 'a great multitude which no one could number, from every nation, from all tribes, and peoples and tongues'" (CCC, no. 1138).

"You have approached Mount Zion and the city of the living God, the heavenly Jerusalem, and countless angels in festal gathering, and the assembly of the firstborn enrolled in heaven" (Heb 12:22-23).

Let us now look further into how the Holy Eucharist celebrated here on earth shows its awareness of its link with the heavenly liturgy.

7. In Union with the Heavenly Host

The Church, in celebrating the Eucharistic sacrifice, is very aware of doing so in union with the heavenly host. One Eucharist Prayer after another confesses: "In union with the whole Church we honor Mary, the ever-virgin Mother of Jesus Christ our Lord and God."[6] Then the following are named: St. Joseph, the Apostles, the martyrs, the confessors, the virgins, and all the saints. "May their merits and prayers," the Church prays at the Eucharistic sacrifice, "gain us your constant help and protection." The Eastern Rite *anaphoras*, or Eucharistic Prayers, do the same.

The angels are given special mention in the Preface. Here are examples. "And so with all choirs of angels in heaven we proclaim your glory and join in their unending hymn of praise" (Advent I); "In our unending joy we echo on earth the song of the angels in heaven as they praise your glory forever" (II Sunday of Lent); "With thankful praise, in company with the angels, we glorify the wonders of your power" (III Sunday of Lent). These references to the angels are only natural, as the cry "Holy, holy, holy" that we make our own immediately afterwards is attributed by Scripture to them (Is 6:3; Rv 4:8).

The Church suffering in purgatory is not forgotten. The Eucharistic sacrifice is also offered for the faithful departed who "have died in Christ but are not yet wholly purified,"[7] so that they may be able to enter into the light and peace of Christ (cf. CCC, no. 1371).

It follows therefore that at the Mass "our union with the heavenly Church is best realized; in the Liturgy, through the sacramental signs, the power of the Holy Spirit acts on us, and with community rejoicing we celebrate together the praise of the divine majesty" (*Lumen Gentium*, no. 50; cf. *Sacrosanctum Concilium*, no. 104). "In the earthly liturgy we take part in a foretaste of that heavenly liturgy which is celebrated in the Holy City of Jerusalem toward which we journey as pilgrims."[8]

8. Eschatological Dimension of the Holy Eucharist

The Holy Eucharist brings us to tend towards the life to come. "For as often as you eat this bread and drink the cup, you proclaim the death of the Lord until he comes," St. Paul tells the Corinthians (1 Cor 11:26). Christ promised his Apostles his own joy, so that their joy may be complete (cf. Jn 15:11). The Eucharist is a foretaste of this joy. It is a confident waiting "in joyful hope for the coming of our Savior, Jesus Christ."[9]

When we receive Jesus in Holy Communion, one of the results is that we get a pledge of eternal life, of our bodily resurrection, since Jesus promised that those who so receive him in this sacrament have eternal life and that he will raise them up at the last day (cf. Jn 6:54). Therefore, St. Ignatius of Antioch called Holy Communion "a medicine of immortality, an antidote to death."[10]

When, therefore, the priest says to us before the Preface, "Lift up your hearts," let us also think of the future life, of heaven, where the Eucharist is bringing us. Pope John Paul II has put it beautifully: "The Eucharist is truly a glimpse of heaven appearing on earth. It is a glorious ray of the heavenly Jerusalem which pierces the clouds of our history and lights up our journey" (*Ecclesia de Eucharistia*, no. 19). "Come, Lord Jesus" (Rv 22:20); "The Spirit and the bride say, 'Come!' Let the hearer say, 'Come'" (Rv 22:17).

9. Eucharist and Commitment to This World

The fact that the Eucharist brings us to long for, to strain or tend towards, the world to come must not be interpreted to imply a diminishing of interest in the improvement of this present world on earth. Quite the contrary.

At the end of Mass the deacon or priest says to us: "*Ite, Missa est*": "Go, our celebration is ended. You are now sent to go and live what we have prayed, and sung and heard. Go to serve God and your neighbor."

The Second Vatican Council is clear on this commitment to improve the Earth:

> The expectancy of a new earth should spur us on, for it is here that the body of a new human family grows, foreshadowing in some way the age which is to come. That is why, although we must be careful to distinguish earthy progress clearly from the increase of the kingdom of Christ, such progress is of vital concern to the kingdom of God, insofar as it can contribute to the better ordering of human society.[11]

Therefore, the Holy Eucharist commits us to undertake initiatives to promote development, justice, and peace. Solidarity and cooperation should replace competition and domination. Oppression, repression, or exploitation of individuals or of the poorer minorities or countries should be eliminated. The Christian who is exiting from the Eucharistic celebration should examine his or her conscience on what can or should be done for the poor, the sick, the handicapped, and the needy in general.

Christ washed the feet of his Apostles to teach them that the Holy Eucharist sends us to actively love our neighbor (cf. Jn 13). St. Paul tells the Corinthians that their participation in the Holy Eucharist is defective if they are indifferent towards the poor (cf. 1 Cor 11:17-22, 27-34). The recent instruction of the Congregation for Divine Worship and the Discipline of the Sacraments stresses this dimension of our participation in the Eucharistic celebration:

> The offerings that Christ's faithful are accustomed to present for the Liturgy of the Eucharist in Holy Mass are not necessarily limited to bread and wine for the eucharistic celebration, but may also include gifts given by the faithful in the form of money or other things for the sake of charity toward the poor. Moreover, external gifts must always be a visible expression of that true gift that God expects from us: a contrite heart, the love of God and neighbor by which we are conformed to the sacrifice of Christ, who offered himself for us.[12]

There is no doubt that the Holy Eucharist commits us to strive to make this world a better place in which to live (cf. *Ecclesia de Eucharistia*, no. 70).

10. Our Response

As we conclude these reflections, we adore and thank our Lord Jesus Christ, who has given us the honor and the possibility of being associated with him in the offering of the Eucharistic sacrifice.

We pray him to teach us to offer ourselves at Mass through him and with him, to make of us an everlasting gift to God the Father.[13] Then the Eucharistic sacrifice becomes for each of us the center of our day and our week, which will all be like an offertory procession. The Eucharist teaches the Church to offer herself. As St. Augustine says, "The Church continues to reproduce this sacrifice in the sacrament of the altar so well-known to believers wherein it is evident to them that in what she offers she herself is offered."[14]

The Holy Eucharist calls on us human beings to be the voice of creation in offering it all to God. The family, work, science and culture, politics and government, the mass media, and recreation, plus sun, moon, trees, rivers, and all created things, should all be offered to God. All creation, redeemed by Christ, should be symbolically offered to God in the Eucharistic sacrifice.

We celebrate the Mass in union with the Blessed Virgin Mary, the angels, and the saints. We pray for the souls suffering in purgatory. We look heavenwards to the time when all those redeemed by Christ will be together to sing for eternity the praises of the Father, the Son, and the Holy Spirit.

Today we pray for the abundant blessings of the Eucharistic Jesus on the Council of Major Superiors of Women Religious and all the members of their religious institutes or congregations. By their consecrated lives they are without words witnessing to Christ and proclaiming "the kingdom of God and its requirements over all earthly things" (*Lumen Gentium*, no. 44). May the Holy Eucharist be the center of their lives, their hopes, their joys.

To Jesus Christ in the Holy Eucharist be honor and glory now and forever.

Reflection Questions

1. In Christ Jesus, heaven and earth are made one. What do the Scriptures concerning the Lamb of God (Jn 1:29, 10:17-28; Rev 5:12), when read alongside the Passover narrative (Ex 12:21-23), tell us about the Holy Eucharist?

2. How does the Holy Eucharist bring about all creation? Does the saving power of the Blood of Christ have any limit of time or space? What does this say of our participation in the Holy Eucharist?

Reflection Questions (continued)

3. How is the heavenly liturgy reflected in the Mass celebrated in the parish church? How is the unity of heaven and earth expressed and brought about by the Sacred Liturgy?

4. Christ washed the feet of his disciplines in the upper room. How are those who celebrate the Eucharist called to wash the feet of others? How might the missionary dimension of the Mass be made clearer?

NOTES

1. Council of Trent, DS 1740; cf. also 1 Cor 11:23; Heb 7:24, 27; *Catechism of the Catholic Church*, no. 1366; *Ecclesia de Eucharistia*, nos. 11, 12.
2. Cf. Council of Trent, DS 1651.
3. *Lumen Gentium*, no. 10.
4. *Roman Missal*, First Christmas Preface.
5. *Ecclesia de Eucharistia*, no. 8.
6. *Roman Missal*, Eucharistic Prayer I.
7. Council of Trent, DS 1743.
8. *Sacrosanctum Concilium*, no. 8; cf. also 1 Cor 15:28; CCC, nos. 1090, 1326.
9. *Roman Missal*, Embolism after the Lord's Prayer.
10. *Ad Ephesios*, 20: PG 5, 661, quoted in *Ecclesiae de Eucharistia*, no. 18; cf. also *Sacrosanctum Concilium*, no. 47.
11. *Gaudium et Spes*, no. 39.
12. *Redemptionis Sacramentum*, no. 70.
13. Cf. *Roman Missal*, Eucharistic Prayer III.
14. *De Civ. Dei*, 10, 6: PL 41, 283; CCC, no. 1372.

BIOGRAPHICAL NOTE

Cardinal Francis Arinze is prefect of the Congregation of Divine Worship and the Discipline of the Sacraments, and he served as the President Delegate of the Eleventh Ordinary General Assembly of the Synod of Bishops, *The Eucharist: Source and Summit of the Life and Mission of the Church*, in October 2005. Cardinal Arinze is a native of Nigeria, where he was ordained a priest in 1958 and spent several years teaching Liturgy and serving as regional secretary for Catholic education. He was ordained a bishop in 1965 and served as Archbishop of Onitsha, Nigeria, until being made president of the Pontifical Council for Interreligious Dialogue. In 1985, he was raised to the dignity of the College of Cardinals. Cardinal Arinze was appointed to his present prefecture in 2002.

CHAPTER 3

Eucharist in the Church and the World

CARDINAL FRANCIS GEORGE

Delivered During the Jubilee Year 2000, at the Forty-Seventh International Eucharistic Congress in Rome, Italy

Some years ago, I was visiting an Oblate missionary in Zambia. He had been living in southern Africa for only a year before I arrived. He was an old friend, and he told me about the country and about the mission and the people that he served on the banks of the Zambesi River. His ministry was a great comfort to him, especially when he was able to celebrate the Eucharist with the people, both in the small mission church and in the villages. His heart was often troubled, however, by the problems of the people: not only as individuals or in families, but also in the society as a whole. Zambia had not adjusted well to the new global economic order. The people he served lived, for the most part, by subsistence farming. A whole generation of young parents were dying of AIDS. The indebtedness of the country meant that education and health care were being curtailed.

After Mass one morning, he returned to the priest's house, and I went to the bank of the river to thank God for the natural beauty of this troubled country. Four men came out of the bush and approached me to ask where they could find the priest. I indicated the house alongside the chapel and three of them went to the door. The fourth stayed with me and we began to talk. I did not speak his language, unfortunately, but he spoke some English. When I asked about his family and work, he repeated many of the difficulties that my friend had already shared with me. Then I asked him why he and his companions had come to speak to the priest. He explained that many stories were heard in his small village, and some of them were about Jesus and the Gospel and the Church. They had come to ask the priest for information about his religion. I then asked him why he was not with his three companions, talking to the priest. He responded, "Oh, I've thought about what we've heard, even while I was walking here, and I've decided it's not for me. It makes no sense when I look at my life—that God would love us, that God would sacrifice himself for us, that God is stronger than the spirits who harm us. I don't believe it. It's too good to be true."

I have thought of this man and prayed for him in the years since that conversation. I do not know if he ever came to believe in the God revealed through Jesus Christ; but what he said was correct. It's too good to be true, except for those whose hearts and minds and souls have been somehow touched and moved by a God who loves us more than we could ever love ourselves, who is closer to us than we are to ourselves.

"The Word became flesh / and made his dwelling among us" (Jn 1:14). The Prologue of the Gospel according to St. John proclaims that the Eternal Logos, the only-begotten Son of God, chose to enter into the very heart of God's temporal creation so that everything can be a sign and invitation to enter into the communal love of God's Trinitarian life. Jesus Christ, our Savior, does not stand apart from creation; he enters into its very life so that all God has accomplished can be seen to exist for the sake of our salvation. Too good to be true? Yes—except for those who, with the eyes of faith, see the world as Christ sees it.

The Scriptures also tell us that the one born of the Virgin Mary, who suffered, died, and is now risen, is Jesus: he was nailed to the cross, has risen from the dead, and lives forever. He has overcome the chains of sin and of death, the ultimate barrier, and now lives in total freedom. Reflect again on the appearances of the Risen Lord to those who knew him best before he was crucified. It is truly Jesus, with the wounds of his crucifixion still visible in his risen body. Nonetheless, he is so different that his clos-est companions often do not recognize him. It is the same Jesus who eats breakfast and supper, and locked doors do not confine him. He comes and goes at will. He is perfectly free.

The Risen Lord, therefore, is free to keep his promise to his disciples: "I am with you always, until the end of the age" (Mt 28:20). The Risen Lord will never abandon his people. Those who find their personal iden-tity in relation to him will never be alone or abandoned. How could they be? The Risen One is wherever he wills to be. Having assumed human nature as the new Adam, he now fills the cosmos as Risen Lord. Too good to be true? Yes—unless one's aspirations have been transformed by the hope of glory in which the Risen Jesus lives and which he offers to us.

This Jesus has also promised, "Where two or three are gathered together in my name, there am I in the midst of them" (Mt 18:20). The

Risen Lord has established a community of believers to be a sign and instrument of salvation, to be the means for God's saving love to transform all creation. When the Church lives visibly through, with, and in her Risen Lord, she is revealed as his living body in every generation. When the Church gathers to celebrate the sacraments, Christ continues to act among us. The Risen Christ baptizes and forgives sin and sends the Holy Spirit to seal our membership in the Church. It is Christ who comforts and heals the sick, who unites a man and woman together for life, and who ordains ministers for the Church. It is Christ who makes present his own self-sacrifice on the cross, so that we can join to it our very selves. Each of the sacraments is an action of the Risen Christ, gathering with his body, the Church.

In a unique fashion, the Eucharist is both the action and the abiding presence of the Lord. In the Eucharist, Christ gives himself as food for our journey, as our daily bread, as a banquet, which bring us together as pilgrims. Christ never comes to us alone. Christ comes to us with the Father and the Holy Spirit. Mary, the Mother of Christ and our mother, accompanies her Son. All the angels and saints, who have gone before us in faith, together with the souls in purgatory join in the great communion. Moreover, all those who are the visible body of Christ throughout the world today are united in the divine gift of love. We, therefore, never go to Jesus alone. In the Eucharist, we are most clearly members of a body, living stones of a temple, a gathered people of God. Too good to be true? Yes—except for those whose hearts have been turned inside out by the unity given to those who know they are loved by God and who have come to sense their unity with the many, who are brothers and sisters of the Risen Lord.

Eucharist in the Life and Thought of the Church

Today, questions of Eucharistic faith and practice are strongly contested in many areas of ecclesial life. Perhaps, at least in the United States, some have been too neglectful of Eucharistic preaching and teaching. Perhaps some have discouraged Eucharistic devotion apart from the celebration of the Mass itself. Perhaps liturgical practice suffers from the lack of prayerful preparation and devout attention. Perhaps some are confused in expressing precisely what the Church teaches about the Holy Eucharist.

Whatever the reason, there is a growing desire among many Catholics for more clarity and insight into our Eucharistic faith and practice. I am grateful for your presence at this International Eucharistic Congress, called by our Holy Father John Paul II. This Eucharistic jubilee celebration gives hope to us all. It expresses our faith and deepens our love in the living presence of Christ among us.

In some ways, contemporary tensions and confusions about the Eucharist should not surprise us. Tension and confusion were there from the beginning: "'This saying is hard; who can accept it?' . . . As a result of this, many [of] his disciples returned to their former way of life and no longer accompanied him" (Jn 6:60, 66). The tension became unbearable when Jesus began to use realistic language about eating his flesh and drinking his blood. In the face of his disciples' confusion, Jesus only intensified his language;[1] he made no attempt to soften or dilute its meaning.

This Eucharistic realism was clearly understood and accepted by the apostolic Church. By sharing in the real, sacrificed, and risen flesh of Christ and in his blood shed on the cross, the Church becomes a living body. Not a body in an organizational or sociological sense; the Church becomes a real body, brought into existence by the Eucharist (1 Cor 10:16ff.).[2] In St. Cyril of Alexandria's words, precisely through the Eucharist, through "eating the flesh of Christ," we are made into a "living flesh." Cyril's realism even compares the union between Christ and the recipient of the Eucharist to a fusion of two globs of sealing wax.[3] Christ desires to be as close to us as nourishment is to our bones.

In the Eucharist, the life of Christ is poured into our lives, that we may have new life as living members of a new body in the world, the body of Christ. St. Ignatius of Antioch (c. AD 110) emphasizes this ecclesial, corporate context of the Eucharist and its attendant gifts. He exhorts the community "animated by one faith and in union with Jesus Christ . . . to show obedience with undivided mind to the bishop and the presbytery, and to break the same Bread, which is the medicine of immortality, the antidote against death, and everlasting life in Jesus Christ" (*To the Ephesians* 20, 2).[4] In fact, for Ignatius, the Eucharist is inseparable from the ministry that gathers people visibly together and is responsible for maintaining Christ's sacramental presence in the Church (*To the Philadelphians*, 4). No one, Ignatius of Antioch says, can (validly) celebrate the Eucharist apart from the bishop, "or anyone to whom he has committed it" (*To the Smyrnaeans* 8, 1).[5]

This inseparable link between Eucharistic realism and ecclesial union gives rise to the great patristic vision of the Eucharist as the bond of charity, unity, and peace: those signs of an authentic civilization of love. St. Augustine, in particular, placed strong emphasis on this "social" function of the Eucharist, "social" in the sense that the bond of love, unity, and peace among the baptized is a participation in the divine *communio* of the Trinitarian life of God. The Eucharist is the secret of the Church's heart and is her comfort in every generation. In this most blessed sacrament, the divine *communio* is disclosed. The Holy Spirit, who works through the Church, makes the Eucharistic elements holy. In the Eucharist, the sacrificial death of Christ is truly present, and its saving power is alive and life-giving. In the Eucharist, the Father is worshiped in spirit and in truth. In the Eucharist, Christ's sacrificial death and Resurrection restores us to the bonds of unity and peace with the Father (justification) and makes possible the outpouring of the Holy Spirit's love into our lives (sanctification).

St. Augustine's central idea is this: through eating Christ's body and drinking his blood, we become one with him and with each other. In Eucharistic *communio,* the City of God, God's great civilization of love, is visible on the earth; for "in what [the Church] offers, she herself is offered" (*De civitate Dei*, X, 6). All of this is possible because Christ is risen from the dead. The Eucharist is his glorified body and blood, which suffered and died, and now shares in the eternity of the celestial Eucharist, "the glory given to the Father by the Son who redeemed the world."[6]

In Catholic consciousness, faith in the Eucharist as embodying and presenting the Risen Christ, who suffered and died for us, must be seen against the background of creation, specifically, a creation leading to Incarnation (Jn 1:1-14; Col 1:15-20). The Creator God enters into his creation and becomes part of it. This presence continues in a Eucharistic and sacramental manner. It is this intrusion of eternity and transcendence into the created world that establishes both the time and the space of the Eucharist.[7] The Eucharist discloses the divine *communio* of Trinitarian love and invites our participation. In this sense, it is a perpetual proclamation of God's transcendence and power, manifested most fully in the life, death, and Resurrection of Jesus Christ the Lord (Phil 2:6-11).

This is true both when the Eucharistic Liturgy is being celebrated and breaks the limits of time and history, and also when the Eucharist is in the tabernacle, where the drama of salvation is not immediately being reenacted, but where Christ is still present for our contemplation and prayer. St. Thomas expresses this contemplative dimension of the

Eucharist in a phrase redolent of Aristotle: "It is the law of friendship that friends should live together" (*Summa theologiae* III, q. 75, a. 1). This is why devotion to the Eucharist, apart from the Eucharistic Liturgy itself, is an indispensable element of Catholic spirituality. It is also why all devotional life should, in some way, be linked to the Eucharist.

In Christ Jesus, the Father desires to dwell in the heart of reality, down to the very depths of our being. The real presence of Christ in the Eucharist is "the presence of the full mystery of God's being and work."[8] Christ accomplishes two things in this sacrament: he glorifies his Father, and he shares his life with us.

The Eucharistic Liturgy as the Locus for Evangelization[9]

The Risen Jesus is the Eucharistic Lord. Free himself, he wants us to be free. Free to do what? We are made free to worship and to glorify God. We are given the freedom to evangelize and convert human hearts and thus to transform the world. The very structure of the Eucharistic Liturgy discloses the dynamics of a new culture.

The Second Vatican Council reminds us that "the Eucharist appears as the source and summit of all preaching of the Gospel."[10] I would suggest that one way of understanding this profound, evangelical depth in the Eucharistic Liturgy is to "track," so to speak, the presence of the Holy Spirit in the Liturgy. It is the Holy Spirit who groans to set us free and who is present in all the decisive moments of Christ's life. In our Savior's Incarnation, life in the world, death, and Resurrection, Jesus is seen doing the Father's will under the guidance, direction, prompting, and assistance of the Holy Spirit.

The New Testament word for invoking the Holy Spirit is *epikalein*, "to call upon/call down." "Calling upon" or "calling down" is an *epiklesis*. Imagine yourselves now at Mass. During the celebration, there are at least eight moments when we explicitly or implicitly call upon the Holy Spirit of God, the Spirit who sets us free and who renews the face of the earth.

Epiklesis of Forgiveness

The first moment is the *epiklesis of forgiveness*. The Penitential Rite is always an implicit invocation of the Holy Spirit because it is a prayer for forgiveness. The Spirit is sent among us for the forgiveness of sins (Jn 20:22-23). This moment of forgiveness is essential to the new culture of Christian life; and, at Jesus' express command, it is essential to Liturgy (Mt 5:23-24).

We must constantly remind ourselves that we are sinners in need of forgiveness. If, as individuals and as a community, we are unaware of our faults, or if we simply ignore them, invariably we cast them into the lives of others, and we have no true claim on God's mercy and forgiveness. Then, the true drama of God's salvation revealed in Jesus Christ is muted; the humility necessary for authentic worship "in Spirit and truth" (Jn 4:23) is undermined. Reconciling love is, thus, the first fruit of the divine *communio*.

Epiklesis of Word

The second moment is the *epiklesis of word*. This refers to the point in the Liturgy when we proclaim directly from Sacred Scripture, which is "inspired by God and is useful for teaching, for refutation, for correction, and for training in righteousness" (2 Tm 3:16). Our profession of faith describes the work of the Spirit: "He spoke through the prophets." We respond to the inspired Scriptures and conform our lives to the teaching of Jesus; but in doing so, we are in fact encountering Jesus through the Spirit that breathes through the Scriptures. The Holy Spirit conforms our lives to the Word of God. The homily, which expounds the Scriptures and relates them directly to the lives of the people in the assembly, is a word integral to Eucharistic worship.

Epiklesis of Intercession

The third moment is the *epiklesis of intercession*. This invocation encompasses the reading of the Scriptures: it begins with the opening prayer and concludes with the General Intercessions. This is another implicit invocation of the Holy Spirit, for the Holy Spirit carries all prayer into the sight of God (Rom 8:26-27). To pray is to accept the grace that changes us. Our spirit, united with the Holy Spirit, enters into the holy drama revealed in Jesus Christ. We are taken into God's saving action in history, where the Holy Spirit transforms our personal and social history.

Prayer itself is a form of instruction and evangelization. Prayer puri-fies our desires; it opens the world to God's transforming action, which waits upon our human freedom. God does not impose himself upon us; we have to ask. Our prayer must, therefore, constantly reach out to the farthest corners of God's creation. It must mourn every human misery and rejoice in every human joy.

Epiklesis of Offering

The next moment is the *epiklesis of offering*. We take two material gifts, bread and wine; and through the power of the Spirit, we ask that they may become "the bread of life" and "our spiritual drink."

On the one hand, these gifts represent ourselves, as we long for ever-greater Eucharistic transformation. The bread represents all our united human efforts that contribute to the building up of a civilization of love on this earth. The wine represents all the pain, suffering, and death involved in the discharge of this holy task—all once again embraced by the Eucharistic Body of the Lord.

On the other hand, the bread and wine represent material creation itself, which awaits its own Eucharistic transformation, a "share in the glorious freedom of the children of God" (Rom 8:21). The Spirit's pres-ence in this moment of offering is often made explicit in the Prayer over the Gifts, which concludes our preparation of the altar and the gifts.

Epiklesis of Consecration

The epiklesis of offering points directly to the next invocation, the *epiklesis of consecration*. The Holy Spirit effects the transformation of the bread and wine into the Body and Blood of the Lord. The word "*consecratio*"—which means "to be holy together with"—carries the most profound sense of the experience of the Holy Spirit in the individual person, in the Church, and in the world. The Holy Spirit is the sanctifier, the one who makes us holy in the sight of God. It is the mission of the Holy Spirit in the world to sanctify, to consecrate each person and community for worship "in Spirit and truth" (Jn 4:24). In the transforming power of consecration, the outpouring of the divine *communio* reveals the clear form of the new culture—a life and world suitable for the indwelling of the trinitarian life of God.

Epiklesis of Memorial

Next is the *epiklesis of memorial*: "Do this in remembrance of me." We do not simply live out of the present; we live with an acute awareness of the past, of all that the Father has done for us in Jesus Christ. When we celebrate this memorial of God's saving action, that saving reality is encountered again through the presence of the Spirit, who brings us into the life of the Risen Lord. In this memorial, the future of the world is anticipated, and the new culture of life is received.

Epiklesis of Communion

The consecration, sanctification, and memorial effected by the Holy Spirit prepare us for the *epiklesis of communion*. Before receiving the Body and Blood of the Lord, we pray, "Lord, I am not worthy to receive you, / but only say the word and I shall be healed" (Roman Liturgy, Communion Rite). This short prayer sums up all the previous moments of epiklesis: forgiveness, word, intercession, offering, and consecration. Communion with the dying and rising Jesus is also communion with the Spirit, who gives life (Rom 8:9-11).

Epiklesis of Mission

The final invocation is the *epiklesis of mission*. The Spirit of God is the energy and dynamism of all mission in the world. "Mission" is the way we live out our baptismal consecration in the world—as married persons; as bishops, priests, and deacons; as single persons; as those consecrated by religious vows—with the energy and prompting of the Holy Spirit.

Having been prepared by the persistent invocation of the Holy Spirit of God, and having been nourished with the Body and Blood of the Lord, the baptized are now sent out, by the power of this same Holy Spirit, to evangelize and to transform society itself. The people of God dwell in this "evangelical form." Together as pilgrims gathered in the Eucharist, we walk every day the journey of forgiveness, of word, of intercession, of offering, of consecration, of communion, and now of mission. What is the context of this mission today? What world is the Eucharist to inform and to transform?

Mission Today

In a world always in search of freedom, we live more and more in a global-ized society. In economics and in politics, in culture and in communica-tion, the human race is more connected than ever before. But a connec-tion is not necessarily a personal relationship. The scope of economic and political activity today brings with it the opportunity of uniting the human family in justice and love. It brings with it as well the danger of an order in which the poor are cut off from participation in the goods of the earth and are unable to enjoy the freedom that God desires for us. Globalization will not be globalization with solidarity unless the Church evangelizes in a new way. It is the Eucharist that gives us the courage to evangelize, because the goal of our human unity is already present in the Eucharist itself. Because of the Eucharist, the Church can be the sacrament of the unity of the human race. In giving himself freely for our salvation and in sending the Holy Spirit, Christ makes us free; but Gospel freedom is greater than the freedom this world understands. In Christ, we are free to act, to do what we need to do, what we should do. The world understands this freedom, the freedom to act; but if free-dom is reduced to actions willed by each of us, the world becomes a brittle place. Each one's freedom is limited by the actions of others; and each action is then negotiated, often in a court of law, so that life becomes a contest of wills.

Freedom in Christ is more than freedom to do. It is also freedom to give totally, even to the point of self-sacrifice, as Christ gave himself to death on the cross. The world understands generosity and often rewards it. The world has a more difficult time understanding self-sacrifice. The crisis in Christian marriage, in consecrated life, and in ordained priest-hood is a crisis of Christian freedom, the freedom to give oneself totally to God, to a spouse, to the Church.

Gospel freedom is freedom to do, freedom to give, and finally free-dom to receive. This dimension of freedom in Christ is even more prob-lematic today, for receiving means admitting we are needy, and no one likes to admit that. Yet if we are not free to receive, we cannot be free in Christ, for in Christ all is gift: the Gospel, the sacraments of the Church, apostolic governance, the Church herself—it is all gift. To be free is to receive the gifts Christ bestows on us. If we are not also free to receive all those whom Christ loves, we are not free in Christ. Each human differ-ence is a gift for all, and it must be welcomed, desired, received by all. In

Christ's body, everyone gives and everyone receives. Everyone has something to share, and everyone is needy.

Freedom to do, freedom to give, freedom to receive—all of this is freedom in Christ, who died and rose to set us free and who calls us to experience this freedom in each Eucharistic celebration, offered for the salvation of the world. Too good to be true? No, not for those who have been set free by Christ and the action of the Holy Spirit in order to be leaven for the whole world. In proclaiming a Eucharistic Lord, we discover again and again who we are and are called to be. It is all gift, but it is all true. "Whoever lives the truth comes to the light, so that his works may be clearly seen done in God" (Jn 3:21).

The Eucharist is the great deed wrought in God. Its truth will be clearly seen when the whole world, through the evangelizing mission of the Church, is a Eucharistic assembly, a new culture of grace, composed of all those whom Christ loves and has set free.

Reflection Questions

1. Cardinal George suggests that the Holy Eucharist is a reality that is "too good to be true . . . unless one's aspirations have been transformed by the hope of glory in which the Risen Jesus lives and which he offers to us." How can we foster Eucharistic faith that is personal, profound, and transforming? What are the obstacles to such a faith in our culture, our parish, and our lives?

2. The cardinal suggests that we may be neglectful of

   - Eucharistic preaching and teaching
   - Eucharistic devotion outside Mass
   - Prayerful preparation for Mass
   - Devout attention at Mass
   - Understanding of the Church's Eucharistic teaching

   What are some concrete ways in which we can remedy these neglects?

Reflection Questions (continued)

3. The "inseparable link between Eucharistic realism and ecclesial union" is often missed by those who experience the Mass as a source of contention and division. How can we help others to experience the celebration of the Eucharist as disclosive of "the divine communion of Trinitarian love"?

4. Reflect on the following eight moments at Mass when we call down the Holy Spirit. How does each change you, and change the Church? How can we foster their effective celebration?

   • Epiklesis of forgiveness
   • Epiklesis of the word
   • Epiklesis of intercession
   • Epiklesis of offering
   • Epiklesis of consecration
   • Epiklesis of memorial
   • Epiklesis of communion
   • Epiklesis of mission

NOTES

1. Note the movement from John 6:44-51 to John 6:53-58. The intensification of language can be seen in the Greek verbs used: first "*phagein*," to eat; but then "*trogein*," to chew or gnaw.

2. H. von Balthasar, *Gottbereites Leben* (Freiburg: Johannes Verlag, 1994), 10.

3. C. Schonborn, *God's Human Face* (San Francisco: Ignatius, 1994), 93; Cyril of Alexandria, *In Iohannis evangelium*, X, 863: *Patrologia Graeca* 74, 341D.

4. Ignatius of Antioch, *To the Ephesians*, 20, 2, in J. A. Kleist, *The Epistles of St. Clement of Rome and St. Ignatius of Antioch* (Westminster, MD: Ancient Christian Writers, 1946), 68.

5. In *The Epistles of St. Clement of Rome and St. Ignatius of Antioch*, 86 and 93.

6. R. Sokolowski, "The Eucharist and Transubstantiation," *Communio* 24 (1997): 870, 869. See Thomas Aquinas, *Summa theologiae* III, 76, q. 5, where Thomas argues that Christ's body is not in the sacrament in the normal way an extended body exists: not as in a place, but purely in the way *substance* is, in the way that substance *is contained* by the dimensions, wherever that substance might be. This is Thomas's understanding of presence *per modum substantiae*.

7. Sokolowski, 873-874.
8. Sokolowski, 873.
9. The material in this section was first developed by Rev. Lawrence Hennessey. See his "The Eucharistic Liturgy as Our Expression of Caring for the Church and the World," *Seminary Journal* 5, no. 3 (1999): 21-33.
10. Second Vatican Council, *Decree on the Ministry and Life of Priests* (*Presbyterorum ordinis*), no. 5, in *Vatican Council II: Volume 1: The Conciliar and Post Conciliar Documents*, edited by Austin Flannery (Northport, NY: Costello Publishing, 1996).

Biographical Note

Cardinal George has served as Archbishop of Chicago since 1997. He presently serves the United States Conference of Catholic Bishops (USCCB) as vice president and has served as chairman of the Bishops' Committee on Liturgy. He also serves as the USCCB representative to the International Commission on English in the Liturgy and as a member of a number of pontifical congregations, including the Congregation for Divine Worship and the Discipline of the Sacraments. He received his PhD from Tulane University in 1970 and a doctorate in sacred theology in Rome at the Pontifical Urban University in 1988.

CHAPTER 4

Theology of the Eucharist

ARCHBISHOP DANIEL PILARCZYK

T he Jubilee Year 2000 was more than just a commemoration of the two-thousandth anniversary of the birth of Jesus. The jubilee also offered an invitation and an opportunity for us to refocus our faith on the basics, to recall what it means to be a Catholic Christian.

The fundamental reality in our jubilee year, that for which we expressed our fundamental thanks during those months, was *salvation.* "God has saved us" is the basic tenet of our faith. For that reason it is necessary to reflect a bit about salvation before we deal with the Eucharist.

Salvation: A Gift from God

"Saving" means keeping something from harm, preserving it from destruction, because of some value or worth that is inherent in it. We save that which has value, and we throw away that which is without value. To say that God has saved us means to say that God has preserved us from destruction, that God has found us to be, or made us to be, worth keeping. The Christian Tradition includes some synonyms for "salvation." One is "redemption," which means buying back from captivity. Another is "justification," which means making someone just or holy. Still another is "sanctification."

To understand what it means to be saved, we have to go back to the very beginning. At its beginning, humanity was in a special relationship with God. God and human beings existed together as friends—not equals, of course, but on a plane of ongoing intimate contact. Human beings at some point decided to try to get along without God, to rely on their own capabilities instead of on God's generosity. This constituted "original sin," which changed the whole tenor of the relationship between God and human beings.

Salvation/redemption/justification/sanctification consists of the healing of this cosmic breach between humanity and God. Salvation was

31

accomplished by a human being who reversed the posture of selfishness and arrogance that our first parents had assumed. This human being, instead of looking out for himself, dedicated his life to obedience to God, to the sharing of himself with others, to consistent dedication to the will of God even when that dedication brought him into conflict with others. This human being was, of course, Jesus, whose whole life of reverence and self-giving was salvific, redemptive, and justifying because it constituted a reversal of human self-seeking—a reversal undertaken not by a run-of-the-mill human being like all the others (one who would have had his own sins to overcome), but one undertaken by a human being who was God ("true God and true man," as the Christian Tradition puts it). This dedication and self-giving to the Father reached its apex in the suffering and death of Jesus, suffering and death caused by the conflict between the consistent dedication of Jesus to the service of his Father and the self-seeking narrowness and hypocrisy of the religious and civic leadership of his time. Jesus' whole life was salvific, but his suffering and death expressed most intensely and clearly the purpose and dedication that lay behind his human existence and the work of his human life.

The Father expressed his acceptance of the life and dedication of Jesus by raising him from the dead, raising him to a new level of life that no human being had ever enjoyed before. This new and glorified existence was a life that would never end and a life that could be shared with other human beings. From the time of the Resurrection, there was a whole new potential in humanity, a potential to share the life of God made available to us in the risen life of Jesus. We are given value and preserved from destruction (i.e., saved); we are brought back from a life of meaninglessness (i.e., redeemed); we are made holy (i.e., justified) to the extent that we participate in the life of the risen Christ: the one human being who lived as God meant human beings to live, the one human being who was God. This participation in God's life that constitutes our salvation comes through God's generosity. It is not something we can earn or deserve. For that reason we refer to God's living and working in us through the life of Christ as "grace": that is, as gratuity and gift.

This is what salvation is all about. The next questions that one might raise are, How does this salvation come to me? How do I participate in it? To answer those questions fully we would have to deal with the nature of revelation and Church, with the function of Sacred Scripture and of the Liturgy, and with the implications of all of those for prayer and personal spirituality. But that is not our purpose here. We limit ourselves to reflecting on the Eucharist and its function in God's gift of salvation.

Three basic realities are involved in the Eucharist, and so three basic aspects of the Eucharist need to be treated if we want to enunciate a reasonably adequate theology of the Eucharist and its role in our salvation. These three realities or aspects of the Eucharist are Eucharist as *sacrifice*, Eucharist as *sacrament*, and Eucharist as *real presence of Christ*.

The Sacraments

But first it is necessary to say a little bit about the sacraments in general. The sacraments are signs and words endowed with the power of Christ. They are the way through which God's people receive the salvation that God offers us. They are the application of the saving action of Christ to people, here and now. In the sacraments, we have present and available to us the salvation that was first offered to humanity through the life and ministry of Christ, through his death and Resurrection. The sacraments, and the Liturgy that constitutes their context, are something that Christ does and that we do with him, not merely as individuals but as the community of the Church that is his body.

Eucharist as Sacrifice

Now we can turn our attention to the Eucharist, and first of all to the Eucharist as a sacrifice. When we celebrate the Eucharist, that is, when we participate in the celebration of Mass, we are taking part in a re-presentation, a re-enactment of Christ's gift of himself that lasted throughout his whole earthly life and that reached its climax in his death on the cross. Christ's saving life and death were not to be one-time events, historical occurrences that took place a long time ago and that we would be invited to remember from a great distance of time. No, Christ's gift of salvation continues to be made present and active in the sacraments, particularly in the sacrifice that is the Eucharist. (Note that a "sacrifice" is a giving of something to God in such a way that it is removed from further purely secular use. Often this removal is symbolized by the destruction of that which is offered.)

In the Eucharistic sacrifice, the Body and Blood of Christ, symbolically separated in the separate consecrations of the bread and wine, are offered once more to the Father, through the action of the priest representing Christ, as they were offered the first time on Calvary. The offering on Calvary expressed in definitive form the faithfulness and obedience of Christ. That same offering that Christ continues to make to his Father in heaven is made present for Christian believers of every age through the Eucharistic offering.

However, this sacrificial offering is not just a renewal of the action of Christ. It also involves the Catholic Christian community. The Church, through the agency of the priest, who represents the people as well as Christ, associates itself with the offering of Christ, so that the sacrifice of praise and thanksgiving is no longer merely that of Christ, but that of his people as well, these people here and now. When we participate in the celebration of the Eucharist, we offer Christ to the Father, but we also offer ourselves, our needs, our gifts, our problems. We "buy in" to the sacrifice of Christ, as it were, so that it is ours as well as his. In the Eucharist we connect with the moment of salvation *par excellence*.

Eucharist as Sacrament

Now let's move on to consider the Eucharist as sacrament, as Holy Communion.

The sacrifices of the Old Law, as well as the sacrifices of paganism, generally involved a sacred meal. The priests and people shared in the sacrifice by eating certain portions of the victim. We share in the sacrifice of Christ by eating and drinking the body and blood of Jesus under the Eucharistic species of bread and wine. Jesus linked his self-sacrifice with this particular kind of eating and drinking at the Last Supper when he called on his apostles to do "this" in memory of him. *This* was the giving of himself in sacrifice, but it was also the sharing in the bread and wine that had become his Body and Blood.

What happens when we receive Holy Communion? First, we receive the living, risen Christ, Body and Blood, soul and divinity. Jesus comes to us not physically as ordinary food does, but in a unique, sacramental way. This presence of Christ in us increases and enlivens our union with the life of the risen Christ. That is, it deepens salvation, redemption, justification in us. Just as physical food strengthens and energizes our bodies, so the Eucharistic food strengthens and energizes our life of grace.

Because Holy Communion deepens the life of Christ in us, it also separates us from sin, both by taking away any small sins that we may be guilty of and by making serious sin less appealing to us.

Because Holy Communion links us more deeply with Christ crucified and risen from the dead, it also puts us into communion with everyone else who shares the life of Christ. There is only one life of the one risen Lord, so all of us who share that life share the lives of each other. That's how we can say that the Eucharist "makes the Church." The Church is the body of Christ, which includes not only Christ himself but also all those who share his life.

Holy Communion also orients us to living out the life of Christ in our ordinary lives. The life of Christ in us is supposed to have practical results, the most basic of which is the extension of the life and action of Christ to the circumstances in which we find ourselves. The risen Christ is more present in the world because we are in contact with him in Holy Communion.

This explains why the Eucharist is the sacrament of social justice: Christ loved the poor, and we are called and empowered to continue his action in our world and in our time.

Eucharist as the Real Presence of Christ

Now let's turn our attention to the final piece of Eucharistic theology: the Eucharist as real presence of Christ.

Our faith teaches that the Eucharistic sacrifice of Christ is not just a symbol, a remembrance of things past such as might be connected with looking at a photograph of a loved one who is long dead. No, it is a real re-presentation of Christ's self-giving. It is the real Christ who continues the self-giving of Calvary—in a different way and in various circumstances, to be sure, but no less really and truly. The sacrifice would lose its force and meaning if Jesus were not really and truly involved in it.

Likewise, receiving Holy Communion is not particularly meaningful if Christ is not really there. When we receive the consecrated bread and wine, we receive the real Christ. The appearances are those of bread and wine, but the reality is Christ, Body and Blood, soul and divinity.

The presence of Christ persists in the sacred species even beyond the time of the Eucharistic celebration. We reserve the Eucharist in our churches. Originally this reservation was to provide Holy Communion to the dying. In later centuries the reserved sacrament has appropriately become the focus of adoration on the part of people who come to make a visit to the Lord.

Conclusion

There is an order in these three aspects of the Eucharist. Before everything else, the Eucharist is the sacrifice of Christ and the Church. The offering of ourselves as Christian community with Christ on the cross is one of the most fundamental responses to the salvation we have received from God. Closely united to the sacrificial offering—in fact an integrating aspect of the offering—is the reception of Holy Communion. Finally, as a consequence of the nature of the Eucharist, we have the real presence of Jesus in our tabernacles.

We do not celebrate the Eucharist mainly to "get Jesus" in Holy Communion, nor in order to make him present for our personal devotion after Mass. We celebrate the Eucharist in order to re-present the self-giving of Jesus that won salvation for us, in order to make our offering of ourselves in union with his offering to the Father, in order to express our thanksgiving to the Father through the gift of ourselves.

The Eucharist is an integrating power that brings together into one every aspect of Christian life. As we have seen, it is a medium by which the fundamental reality that is salvation is brought into contact with these people in this place in this time. It also unites us with all those who live the life of Christ in the present, whether the present of time or the present of eternity. In strengthening our membership with Christ, we strengthen our solidarity with everyone else who lives in him. Because the Eucharist offers and expresses the very center of Christian belief, participation in the Eucharist constitutes a profession of our Catholicity, of the one faith we all share. (This is why persons who do not fully share our faith should not receive the Eucharist in our churches. They would be professing a unity of faith commitment that they do not intend.)

Similarly, because the Eucharist is an integrating force, an energy that expresses and deepens wholeness, those whose lives are unintegrated because of serious, ongoing sinfulness cannot fruitfully receive the Eucharist without first re-integrating themselves with God through the sacrament of reconciliation. You cannot celebrate wholeness if your spirit is fragmented and self-contradictory.

The Eucharist is also an integrator of time. Past, present, and future are united in the one focal point of the sacrifice of Jesus. This sacrifice first took place in the past when Jesus suffered and died under Pontius Pilate. But it is brought into present contact with us through the presence and action of the risen Christ, glorious in majesty with his Father in heaven. And it directs us toward and prepares us for a future when there will be a new heaven and a new earth, when we will all be together with Christ in the presence of Father and Holy Spirit.

"Christ has died. Christ is risen. Christ will come again." That's what salvation is all about. That's what we celebrate in the Eucharist.

Reflection Questions

1. Archbishop Pilarczyk speaks of salvation as "the healing of the cosmic breach between humanity and God" through the obedience of Jesus on the cross. Do we, as individuals and as members of modern culture, appreciate the need for salvation?

2. Christ joins the Church to the sacrifice of himself upon the cross in the celebration of the Holy Eucharist. How does this holy action "make the Church"?

3. The presence of Christ continues even beyond the celebration of the Holy Eucharist in the Eucharistic species reserved in the tabernacle. How can this perduring presence of Christ lead us to a deeper participation in the celebration of the sacrament and sacrifice?

BIOGRAPHICAL NOTE

Archbishop Pilarczyk has been the archbishop of Cincinnati since 1982. He served from 1989 to 1992 as the President of the then-National Conference of Catholic Bishops. Currently a member of Bishops' Committee on the Liturgy, he was its chairman from 1984 to 1986. He was also a member of the International Commission on English in the Liturgy from 1987 to 1997 and was its chairman from 1991 to 1997. Archbishop Pilarczyk obtained a PhL and a doctorate in sacred theology from the Pontifical Urban College in 1956 and 1961, respectively, and a PhD from the University of Cincinnati in 1969.

CHAPTER 5

Eucharist and Trinity

Fr. J. Augustine DiNoia, OP

A Community Called by God

Americans are great joiners. In a variety of clubs, fraternities, unions, alliances, movements, and societies, we join with other people who share our social background, interests, or goals. We are always in danger of thinking of the Church as if it were just another organization we decide to join and support—often by consciously embracing an allegiance that is no more than an accident of our birth into a particular family. Seen in this way, our participation in the Church's life does not look very different from our participation in other kinds of voluntary or professional associations. After all, so much of the Church's day-to-day life depends on us: our attendance, our response, our support, our devotion, our readiness to volunteer. This way of thinking is abetted by the typically American penchant for forming new denominations and church communities. Our "religious affiliation" is just one more item in our personal profiles.

When we think of the Church in this way, the Eucharist can appear to be little more than a celebration of our fellowship with like-minded people drawn together by their desire to give religious expression to their deepest feelings and by their need to find communal legitimation for their morally earnest commitments. God is indeed to be worshiped in this celebration, but almost as an afterthought. What can become primary in this mindset is the celebration of our being together—our fellowship, our solidarity, our communal identity.

But to think in this way about the Church and the Eucharist is to miss a very important truth. Well before we ever thought of belonging to the Church or of sharing in the Eucharist, the Father, Son, and Holy Spirit conceived a plan that would join us to them and to one another in them. Indeed, St. Paul declares that "before the foundation of the world" (Eph 1:4) this plan was already in place. There is a Church only because the triune God has gathered a chosen people to himself. We are members of this Church only because we have been claimed by Christ and baptized

39

in the Holy Spirit. Our participation in the Eucharist brings us into what is, as Pope John Paul II said, nothing less than the "*sacramentum unitatis* which profoundly marks the Church as a people gathered 'by' and 'in' the unity of the Father, of the Son and of the Holy Spirit."[1]

A Trinitarian Communion

The foundation for the visible communion of the Church—for our fellowship with one another—is the invisible communion with the Father, Son, and Holy Spirit that is God's gift to us in Baptism and that sanctifying grace makes possible. The *Catechism of the Catholic Church* (CCC) says that the Church is the sacrament of this trinitarian communion.[2]

The whole of the sacramental and liturgical life of the Church is directed to fostering our participation in this blessed communion. Indeed, as we shall see, the sacramental and liturgical life of the Church—notably the Eucharist itself—has a deep, underlying trinitarian structure. The Church's Liturgy expresses the truth that everything in creation and redemption comes from the Father, through the Son, and in the Holy Spirit, so that in the power of the Holy Spirit, through the Son, all things might return to the Father. This absolutely fundamental Christian truth is captured in the ancient formula: *a Patre, per Filium eius, Jesum Christum, in Spiritu Sancto, ad Patrem.* This pattern is crucial for a proper understanding of and an effective participation in the Eucharist.

To be sure, our belonging to the Church entails a free act on our part—it must be free if it is to be truly personal. But it is also true that this is a *divinely enabled* free act that brings us a share in a communion with the triune God and with one another in him that is itself a *divine gift*. God enables us to do freely what we would be unable to do without his grace. Our membership and participation in the Church is already a membership in the divine "family" of the uncreated Persons and a participation in the divine life. In the Catholic understanding, the formation of the Church is in the first place a divine initiative and action. We have become part of something that exists prior to our interests, determinations, plans, and objectives.

In Baptism, we are washed cleaned "in the name of the Father, and of the Son, and of the Holy Spirit"; we are made to share in the communion of the Blessed Trinity as partakers of the divine life and thus as members of the visible and hierarchically constituted community of persons—the Church—that flows from God and rests in him. The Eucharist begins with the invocation of the Blessed Trinity. Immediately there follows a greeting addressed to us by the priest acting *in persona Christi capitis* and thus, in effect, by the triune God himself: "The grace of our Lord Jesus Christ and the love of God and the fellowship of the Holy Spirit be with you all." Signed and greeted by the all-holy triune God, we settle down to confess our unworthiness and, apart from Christ and the Spirit, our unfitness to enjoy this sacrificial banquet. If there is—as indeed there is—a fellowship to enjoy and celebrate in the Eucharist, it is constituted in the first place by the grace and mercy of the triune God, not by us. We have been invited from the highways and byways to be guests at a wedding banquet that we did not prepare and in which our participation is confirmed only by our being suitably clothed in Christ, in robes "washed . . . in the blood of the Lamb" (Rev 7:14; see Mt 22:1-14).

God in effect announced to Israel after the Exodus from Egypt: you were no people before you were my people. The Church is a creation of the triune God: from the Father, who sends his Son and his Spirit to transform creaturely persons so that they come to share, with the uncreated Persons of the Trinity and with one another, a communion of divine life. Coming from the Father, through the Son, and in the Holy Spirit, the Church is the body of Christ and the temple of the Holy Spirit. "For just as the power of Christ's sacred flesh unites those in whom it dwells into one body," wrote St. Cyril of Alexandria, "in the same way the one and undivided Spirit of God, who dwells in all, leads all into spiritual unity" (cited in CCC, no. 738). The Church's faith in God is a faith in the triune God revealed to us by Christ and fully manifested on the day of Pentecost—the day on which the Church came to be by the power of the Holy Spirit.

Drawn into the Life of the Triune God

In a deeply mysterious way, the Church draws upon and is drawn into the life of the Blessed Trinity itself.

The Father, Son, and Holy Spirit are equally, consubstantially, and indivisibly one God, yet they are distinct by reason of their relations. The Father, who is without origin and who is the source of the inner divine life, begets the Son, who shares the fullness of divinity but not the property of being the Father. "For just as the Father has life in himself, so also he gave to his Son the possession of life in himself" (Jn 5:26). The Father and the Son give themselves to one another with a perfect love from which the Holy Spirit proceeds. The Father, Son, and Holy Spirit are equally God, yet they are distinct. Here is distinction without division, taking origin without inequality. The communion of trinitarian life is the communion of three persons in power, wisdom, goodness, and perfect love.

By the gracious and loving design of this triune God, creaturely persons are destined before the foundation of the world to share in this communion of divine life, a communion that properly belongs only to the uncreated Persons. Because the triune God desires to share this divine life with persons who are not God, he has brought the whole created order into existence. Apart from this divine desire and undertaking, nothing would exist—neither angels nor material universe, neither galaxies nor solar systems, neither Sun nor Earth, neither plants nor animals nor humans.

Into this world, the Father sends the Son and the Holy Spirit to bring all things back to God. "Blessed be the God and Father of our Lord Jesus Christ, who has blessed us in Christ with every spiritual blessing . . . as he chose us in him, before the foundation of the world . . . he destined us for adoption to himself through Jesus Christ . . . sealed with the promised holy Spirit, which is the first installment of our inheritance" (Eph 1:3-5, 13-14). Our participation in this inner trinitarian life is accomplished through Christ and in the Holy Spirit. How does this happen? The action of Christ and the Holy Spirit overcomes the obstacles that arise both from our creatureliness and our sinfulness.

As persons created in the image of God, we are capable of knowing and loving other persons. But in order to know and love not only other persons like ourselves but also Persons who are God, we need to be transformed and empowered by grace. By the power of the Holy Spirit, Christ was born of the Virgin Mary and became man in order that we might become sharers in the divine life. In the words of the prayer over the gifts at Christmas midnight mass, "By our communion with God made man, may we become more like him who joins our lives to yours."

But not only our creaturely natures must be transformed by grace if we are to become "share[rs] in the divine nature" (2 Pt 1:4). Unless our sins are washed away and we become reconciled with God, how can we become sharers in the triune God's most holy life? "Blessed be the God and Father of our Lord Jesus Christ, who in his great mercy gave us a new birth to a living hope through the Resurrection of Jesus Christ from the dead, to an inheritance that is imperishable, undefiled, and unfading, kept in heaven for you" (1 Pt 1:3-4). Christ is victorious over the sin and death that would prevent us from sharing the communion of trinitarian life for which God has destined us in love. In the consummation of the Paschal Mystery, the risen Christ sends his Holy Spirit into us to bring about our transformation—our sanctification—in the image of the only-begotten Son.

Through Christ and in the power of the Holy Spirit, our creatureliness is transformed (*gratia elevans*, or elevating grace) and our sinfulness is healed (*gratia sanans*, or healing grace) so that we can share in the communion of trinitarian life. Thus, it becomes clear that our participation in this divine life mirrors the pattern of the trinitarian processions and missions—but in reverse. In God, from the Father's love of his only-begotten Son, there bursts forth the Holy Spirit. In us, by the power of the Holy Spirit, we are transformed in the image of Christ and thus become beloved of the Father. Hence we pray to the Father, "You sent him as one like ourselves, though free from sin, that you might see and love in us what you see and love in Christ" (Preface VII for the Sundays of Ordinary Time). The trinitarian structure of our transformation in grace is evident in this striking passage from St. Irenaeus: "It is impossible to see God's Son without the Spirit, and no one can approach the Father without the Son, for the knowledge of the Father is the Son, and the knowledge of God's Son is obtained through the Holy Spirit" (cited in CCC, no. 683).

Liturgy Expresses the Trinity

The cycle of the whole liturgical year expresses this radically trinitarian pattern: the Father sends his Son, who was born of the Virgin Mary by the power of the Holy Spirit (Advent–Christmas–Epiphany); who for our sake suffered, died, and was buried; who on the third day rose again in fulfillment of the Scriptures, ascended into heaven, and is seated at the right hand of the Father (Lent–Passiontide–Easter); and who sends the Holy Spirit who proceeds from the Father and the Son (Pentecost). Our return to the Father replicates and reverses this pattern.

From the introductory rites to the final blessing, the Eucharistic Liturgy reflects the fundamental trinitarian structure of the economy of salvation as it comes from the Father, through the Son, and in the Holy Spirit and returns in the power of the Holy Spirit and through the Son to the Father. Almost all of the orations (Opening Prayers, Prayers over the Gifts, and Prayers After Communion), as well as the Prefaces and the great Eucharistic Prayers, are addressed to the Father, through the Son, and in the Holy Spirit. Indeed, the entire Eucharistic celebration follow this basic pattern from beginning to end. This pattern is especially evident in the Eucharistic Prayers. Everything here comes from the Father and is directed to the Father. The incarnate Son is the high priest through whom we perform the same priestly action. The prayer of consecration involves a solemn invocation of the Holy Spirit, by whose power the death and Resurrection of Christ are made present, and the bread and wine are transformed into his Body and Blood. Then, by worthily consuming the Body and Blood of Christ, the faithful are made divine and brought into union with the Father and with one another, through Christ and in the power of the Holy Spirit. Holy Communion thus confirms and nourishes the communion with the Father, Son, and Holy Spirit that God wills to accomplish in his grace and mercy.

But this is not the end. After the final blessing—conferred "in the name of the Father, and of the Son, and of the Holy Spirit"—the faithful are sent forth to "undertake with the strength of the Risen Lord and his Spirit *the tasks which await them in their ordinary life*" (*Dies Domini*, no. 45). The Eucharist is called the "Mass" ("*missa*") precisely to signal the mystery of our being sent forth (*missio*) to fulfill God's will in our daily lives (CCC, no. 1332). In this connection, Pope John Paul II stated that "the Prayer after Communion and the Concluding Rite—the Final Blessing and the Dismissal—need to be better valued and appreciated, so that all who have shared in the Eucharist may come to a deeper sense of the responsibility which is entrusted to them" (*Dies Domini*, no. 45). Again, a trinitarian pattern is evident. The missions of the Son and Spirit are temporal prolongations of their eternal processions. The Father sends the Son and the Spirit, and now the Son sends us out in the Spirit.

Only in the light of our vocation to share in the life of the Father, Son, and Holy Spirit, and to enjoy communion with one another in them, can we fully grasp the nature of the Church and the place of the Eucharist in our lives. No wonder, then, that the Fathers of the Second Vatican Council proclaimed that from Pentecost onward,

> the Church has never failed to come together to celebrate the paschal mystery, reading those things "which were in all the scriptures concerning him" (Lk 24:27), celebrating the eucharist in which "the victory and triumph of his death are again made

present" [Council of Trent, Decree on the Holy Eucharist, ch. 5], and at the same time "giving thanks to God for his unspeakable gift" (2 Cor 9:15) in Christ Jesus, "in praise of his glory" (Eph 1:12), through the power of the Holy Spirit.[3]

Further Reading

Bouyer, Louis. *Eucharist: Theology and Spirituality of the Eucharistic Prayer.* Translated by Charles Underhill Quinn. Notre Dame, IN: University of Notre Dame Press, 1968.

DiNoia, J. Augustine, OP, et al. *The Love That Never Ends: A Key to the Catechism of the Catholic Church.* Huntington, IN: Our Sunday Visitor Press, 1996.

Fatula, Mary Ann, OP. *The Triune God of Christian Faith.* Collegeville, MN: Liturgical Press, 1990.

Forte, Bruno. *He Loved Them to the End: Theological Meditations on Love and Eucharist.* Translated by Robert D. Paolucci. Boston: St. Paul Books and Media, 1993.

Marshall, Bruce. *Trinity and Truth.* New York: Cambridge University Press, 2000.

O'Donnell, John J., SJ. *The Mystery of the Triune God.* London: Sheed and Ward, 1989.

Paul VI. *Mysterium Fidei* (*The Mystery of Faith*) (1965). http://www.vatican. va/holy_father/paul_vi/encyclicals/documents/hf_p-vi_enc_03091965_ mysterium_en.html.

Sacred Congregation of Rites. *Eucharisticum Mysterium* (*Instruction on the Worship of the Eucharistic Mystery*) (1967). In *Vatican Council II: Volume 1: The Conciliar and Post Conciliar Documents.* New rev. ed. Edited by Austin Flannery. Northport, NY: Costello Publishing, 1996.

Vagaggini, Cipriano, OSB. *Theological Dimensions of the Liturgy.* Collegeville, MN: Liturgical Press, 1976.

Reflection Questions

1. How is our role in the Church different from being a member of a club? What does it mean to say that the Eucharist is the sacrament of unity?

2. What does it mean that the priest, acting in the person of Christ, greets us with the words "The grace of our Lord Jesus Christ and the love of God and the fellowship of the Holy Spirit be with you all"?

3. How does God make us one with the life of the Blessed Trinity? How can you personally deepen your appreciation of this reality in the celebration of the Holy Eucharist?

NOTES

1. John Paul II, *On Keeping the Lord's Day Holy* (*Dies Domini*) (1998), no. 36, http://www.vatican.va/holy_father/john_paul_ii/apost_letters/documents/hf_jp-ii_apl_05071998_dies-domini_en.html. Cf. St. Cyprian, *De Orat. Dom.* 23: PL 4, 553; *De Cath. Eccl. Unitate*, 7: CSEL 31, 215. See also Second Vatican Council, *Dogmatic Constitution on the Church* (*Lumen Gentium*), no. 4; *Constitution on the Sacred Liturgy* (*Sacrosanctum Concilium*), no. 26.

2. *Catechism of the Catholic Church*, 2nd ed. (Washington, DC: United States Conference of Catholic Bishops–Libreria Editrice Vaticana, 2000), no. 738. Hereafter cited in text as CCC. For more on the material covered in this chapter, see especially nos. 198-810, 1077-1112, 1322-1419.

3. Second Vatican Council, *Sacrosanctum Concilium* (*Constitution on the Sacred Liturgy*) (1963), no. 6, http://www.vatican.va/archive/hist_councils/ii_vatican_council/documents/vat-ii_const_19631204_sacrosanctum-concilium_en.html.

BIOGRAPHICAL NOTE

Fr. DiNoia is undersecretary of the Congregation for the Doctrine of the Faith. Ordained a Dominican priest in 1970, he previously served as the executive director of the Secretariat for Doctrine and Pastoral Practices of the United States Conference of Catholic Bishops from 1993 to 2001, when he became director of the Intercultural Forum at the Pope John Paul II Cultural Center. He holds his pontifical license in theology from the Dominican House of Studies and received a PhD from Yale University in 1980.

CHAPTER 6

Sunday and the Eucharistic Celebration

MSGR. JAMES P. MORONEY

E ach Catholic family is called upon to remember Sunday as a special day: a day of rest, of charity, and of prayer—and, at the center of it all, a day for Sunday Mass. While in our own day the
people of these United States are challenged as never before to keep holy
the Lord's day, we must never lose sight of the heroic passion that has
joined countless faithful men and women to Sunday Mass throughout
the ages.

In his landmark apostolic letter *Dies Domini* (*On Keeping the Lord's
Day Holy*), Pope John Paul II recalled the example of the martyrs of Abi-
tina, in Proconsular Africa. Interrogated before the tribunal about their
religious practices, they were recorded as responding, "Without fear of
any kind we have celebrated the Lord's Supper, because it cannot be
missed; that is our law . . . we cannot live without the Lord's Supper."[1]

This testament of faith echoes the Lord's words proclaimed during
Sunday Mass: *Unless you eat the flesh of the Son of Man and drink his blood
you will have no life in you.* "We cannot live without the Lord's Supper"
(*Dies Domini*, no. 46).

While I could have made these remarks a reflection on the nature
of obligation in the Church in the United States, the role of the family in
fulfilling this precept, the importance of Sunday Vespers, or any number
of other dimensions of this pastoral challenge, I have chosen to reflect
on Sunday and the Eucharist. This topic is particularly appropriate when
we listen both to what our Holy Father John Paul II has said about the
celebration of Sunday Eucharist in his apostolic letter letter *Dies Domini*
and to the recently revised *Missale Romanum*.

The Sunday Eucharist: What It Is

At the heart of *Dies Domini* is an extended description of the Sunday Eucharist: both what it is and how we can make it a more effective manifestation of what it is supposed to be.

The Holy Father John Paul II described Sunday Mass as a paradigm of Sunday: a paradigm of what it means to be the *dies Domini* and what it means to be the *dies Ecclesiae.*

We are told that Sunday Mass is a paradigm of what it means to be the *dies Domini* because the Mass is the celebration of the sacrifice through which the Lord redeemed the world, the same world that was made through him and that in him will be made one at the end of time. Sunday, therefore, is about the Lord: "Christian believers should come together, in order to commemorate the suffering, Resurrection and glory of the Lord Jesus, by hearing God's Word and sharing the Eucharist, and to give thanks to God who has given them new birth to a living hope through the Resurrection of Jesus Christ from the dead (cf. 1 Pt 1:3)" (*Dies Domini*, no. 8).

But the *dies Domini* is also the *dies Ecclesiae* (*Dies Domini*, no. 35), which is why the Sunday Mass is the paradigmatic *sacramentum unitas*. Never is the Church more called to be one than at the Sunday celebration of the Eucharist. Here mothers and fathers with children in tow gather with widows and singles, the old and the young, the joyful and the mourning, the enfeebled and the strong, the virtuous and the sinners, all made one in a great *sacrificium laudis*, all gathered to the cross by Christ.

Nor is this celebration circumscribed by the walls of the Church in which we gather. For as the new *Roman Missal* tells us, the Sunday Mass is both "the center of the whole Christian life for the Church both universal and local" and a manifestation of the universal Church.[2]

We face so many challenges when we seek to celebrate Sunday Mass as a *sacramentum unitas*:

- When divisions of language and culture seem to necessitate the division of the Church into language or cultural groups
- When a certain consumerist mentality urges the marketing of the early morning Mass as ideal for golfers (the one short one with no singing), the vigil as custom-made for the elderly, the children's nine o'clock Mass, and the noontime choir Mass

- When the terrible divisions of progressive and traditional, of kneelers and standers, hand-folders and hand-holders, and every other imaginable permutation make the Sunday Mass the forum for division and the battlefield of competing visions

At such times, the Sunday Mass is often perceived as more a *sacramentum deintigratis* than a *sacramentum unitatis*.

It is an enormous challenge for pastors and faithful to make the Sunday Mass the most concrete manifestation of the *dies Ecclesiae*. Thus did Pope John Paul II recall that while "it is normal to find different groups, movements, associations and even the smaller religious communities present in the parish," on Sunday "small group Masses are not to be encouraged," in order "that the life and unity of the Church community are fully safeguarded and promoted" (*Dies Domini*, no. 54).

The Eschatalogical Dimension of the Dies Ecclesiae

A second aspect of the Sunday Mass as manifestation of the *dies Ecclesiae* is a realization of the eschatological character of Sunday Mass. The Sunday gathering of a pilgrim people manifests the eschatological character of the Church, as the Church "moves towards the final *Lord's Day*, that Sunday which knows no end" (*Dies Domini*, no. 37).

> Gathering her children into the Eucharistic assembly and teaching them to wait for the "divine Bridegroom," [the Church] engages in a kind of "exercise of desire" ("*Haec est vita nostra, ut desiderando exerceamu*": St. Augustine, *In Prima Ioan. Tract.* 4, 6: SC 75, 232), receiving a foretaste of the joy of the new heavens and new earth, when the holy city, the new Jerusalem, will come down from God, "prepared as a bride adorned for her husband" (Rev 21:2). (*Dies Domini*, no. 37)

Thus, the *Dies ecclesiae* is also a *spei dies* in anticipation of the wedding feast of the Lamb. It is the day that transcends all time and space, a "leaven and the light of human hope" (*Dies Domini*, no. 38).

At this point I might note that the eschatological and universal dimensions of this hope are often missing from our celebrations of the Sunday Liturgy. How often are the Prayers of the Faithful centered not on the needs of the whole world but on the wants of a particular parish.

How often do homilies center more upon the trite, the transitory human emotion, and the banal rather than on the blessed hope of all humanity, the transcendent truth of all time, and the reality of the Church "as a sacrament, or sign and instrument of intimate union with God and of the unity of the entire human race" (*Lumen Gentium*, no. 1, as cited in *Dies Domini*, no. 38).

The Sunday Eucharist: An Assessment

Understanding what the Sunday Eucharist is, as the paradigm of *dies Domini* and *dies Ecclesiae*, we might well ask ourselves, How can we make the Sunday celebration of the Eucharist more responsive to its identity?

In his apostolic letter, Pope John Paul II invited us to an examination of conscience of sorts in relationship to several aspects of Sunday Mass. Allow me to briefly address each in turn.

1. Liturgy of the Word

The first challenge given to pastors and liturgists by the Holy Father in *Dies Domini* is found in paragraph 40: "In considering the Sunday Eucharist more than thirty years after the Council, we need to *assess how well the word of God is being proclaimed* and how effectively the People of God have grown in knowledge and love of Sacred Scripture" (my emphasis; the Second Vatican Council's *Constitution on the Sacred Liturgy*, *Sacrosanctum Concilium*, speaks of "*suavis et vivus Sacrae Scripturae affectus*," no. 24). The Holy Father went on to say that this reassessment has two aspects: the proclamation and the approbation of the Word of God. His challenge is not dissimilar to what we hear in the introduction to the revised *Lectionary for Mass*, when it quotes from St. Jerome: "Not to know the scriptures is not to know Christ."

The encounter with the word is an encounter with the Lord, and proclaiming that word is proclaiming the Lord. Knowing that word is knowing him. Being transformed by that word is being transformed by him. Being made into the image of that word is being made into his image. Hear the Council Fathers almost forty years ago: the Scriptures "present *God's own Word in an unalterable form*, and they make the voice of the Holy Spirit sound again and again in the words of the prophets and apostles. . . . In the sacred books the Father who is in heaven comes lovingly to meet his children, and talks with them" (my emphasis).[3]

Our reading, proclaiming, and hearing the Word of God, then, is an intimate encounter between God and his people. The Father, speaking his Eternal Word, made flesh in our time: reaching down from heaven into our earthly existence and speaking with us, teaching us the mysteries of life.

And precisely because of the intimacy of this encounter between God and his beloved children, the Word of God can never be properly read by the eyes alone, or heard by the ears alone. It is, to paraphrase a famous author, "only with the heart that one hears rightly." Pope John Paul II once spoke of this in an *ad limina* talk to the bishops of the northwestern United States:

> Active participation certainly means that, in gesture, word, song and service, all the members of the community take part in an act of worship, which is anything but inert or passive. Yet active participation does not preclude the active passivity of silence, stillness and listening: indeed, it demands it. Worshipers are not passive, for instance, when listening to the readings or the homily, or following the prayers of the celebrant, and the chants and music of the liturgy. These are experiences of silence and stillness, but they are in their own way profoundly active. In a culture which neither favors nor fosters meditative quiet, the art of interior listening is learned only with difficulty. Here we see how the liturgy, though it must always be properly inculturated, must also be counter-cultural.[4]

Preparation for the proclamation of the word of God is, then, not just the job of the well-trained deacon lector. Proclamation of the word of God is the job of each one of us, involved in an intimate dialogue—not just between reader and congregation, not just between deacon and congregation, not just between priest and congregation, but a dialogue between God and his Church, between your heart and the Sacred Heart of Christ: *Cor ad cor loquitur.*

Knowledge of the word is not simply a matter of comprehending liturgical law or scriptural science, as necessary as such an understanding may be. As the Council Fathers reminded us, something more is needed. We must know the Liturgy "by heart." We must break open the word proclaimed and the prayers prayed of our rite and allow it to form us. We must pray the Sunday readings in the quiet of our room before hearing it in the gathered assembly. Only when it has become a part of the fiber of our being and the rhythm of our day will the word of Scripture proclaimed at the Liturgy begin to transform and consecrate us from deep within our being. And only when the word has transformed us will it transform the Church so badly in need of "that full, conscious, and active participation" demanded by the very nature of the Liturgy.

2. Liturgy of the Eucharist

The second area of Sunday Mass that the Holy Father asked us to reexamine is the Liturgy of the Eucharist, wherein the people of God recall the daily sacrifices of their lives and—grateful for the blessings of God during the past week—are drawn into the Liturgy, willingly lifting up their hearts and making themselves one with the offering of the Priest, which is the sacrifice of Christ himself, through whom, with whom, and in whom is all glory God to God for all ages. (See *Dies Domini*, nos. 42-43.)

It is this "ascending" participation in the sacrifice of Christ which is the source and summit of the entire Christian life. This is what the new *Roman Missal* means when it describes the celebration of Mass as "the high point both of the action by which God sanctifies the world in Christ and of the worship that the human race offers to the Father, adoring him through Christ, the Son of God, in the Holy Spirit" (GIRM, no. 16; see *Sacrosanctum Concilium*, no. 10). In an earlier liturgical book, the Church is even more explicit: "The celebration of the Eucharist is the center of the entire Christian life, both for the Church universal and for the local congregations of the Church."[5]

From this celebration of the Eucharist derive the various manifestations of the presence of Christ, including the perduring presence of Christ in the Eucharistic species. In the years since the Council, we have done marvelous work in appreciating the manifestations of the presence of Christ in the Liturgy. We have opened wide the doors on the treasury of Sacred Scripture with the reform of the *Lectionary for Mass* and have situated the proclamation of God's word at the heart of each of the reformed liturgical rites.

Likewise, the essential role of the congregation gathered for worship and the presence of Christ among those who gather in his name have led to a recognition of the many and varied ministries of the Body of Christ and the "full, conscious, and active participation" of the faithful that was so highly recommended by the Council Fathers.[6]

The presence of Christ in the priest who convenes the assembly *in persona Christi* has been a bit more of a challenge for us, as witnessed by the 2004 interdicasterial instruction on the Eucharist, *Redemptionis Sacramentum*, and by the crisis of delineation of roles of clergy and laity. However, only in recent years have we begun a more critical reflection on the ultimate presence of Christ, described by the Council Fathers as his presence *par excellence*: the presence of Christ in the Eucharistic species.

Since the Council we have been blessed with an extended reflection on the worship of the Eucharistic mystery by Pope Paul VI (*Mysterium Fidei* [*The Mystery of Faith*]), the liturgical book *Holy Communion and Worship of the Eucharist Outside of Mass*, and the apostolic letter *Ecclesia de Eucharistia* (*On the Eucharist*) of Pope John Paul II[7] to aid us in discovering the role of Eucharistic worship in the life of the parish and the life of the Church. These important documents teach that a major part of this same tradition of praying in the presence of God is the reservation and adoration of the Eucharist is our churches, a tradition presently witnessing a resurgence in many places. The establishment of extended periods of adoration can be of significant support to the spiritual and sacramental life of every parish.

From the beginning, however, both priests and the faithful must keep in mind the dynamic relationship between Eucharistic adoration and Mass itself. The former is the gift of the latter, and authentic Eucharistic adoration leads to a fuller, more conscious, and active participation in the Mass, which is the source and the summit of the entire Christian life.

This is why the Bishops' Committee on the Liturgy will issue a resource in the form of a series of questions and answers on this important aspect of the Church's life (entitled *Thirty-One Questions on Adoration of the Blessed Sacrament*).[8] The resource seeks to foster the same appreciation of Eucharistic adoration that Pope Paul VI articulated some thirty-six years ago:

> the devotion which leads the faithful to visit the Blessed Sacrament draws them into an ever deeper participation in the Paschal Mystery. It leads them to respond gratefully to the gift of him who through his humanity constantly pours divine life into the members of his body (Decree on the Ministry and Life of Priests, no. 5: AAS 58 [1956], pp. 997-999). Dwelling with Christ our Lord, they enjoy his intimate friendship and pour out their

hearts before him for themselves and their dear ones, and pray for the peace and salvation of the world. They offer their entire lives with Christ to the Father in the Holy Spirit, and receive in this wonderful exchange an increase of faith, hope and charity. Thus they nourish those right dispositions which enable them with all due devotion to celebrate the memorial of the Lord and receive frequently the bread given us by the Father.[9]

3. Holy Communion

In their 2002 *Norms for the Distribution and Reception of Holy Communion Under Both Kinds for the Dioceses of the United States of America*,[10] the bishops of the United States recalled that while "sharing in the Lord's Supper is always communion with Christ," it is in the reception of Holy Communion that the "the consummation of the Mass is found . . . whereby the people purchased for the Father by his beloved Son eat and drink the Body and Blood of Christ" (no. 5).

In this regard, I recommend to your study the theological introduction to the *Norms*. Therein the act of Holy Communion is described as union with Christ present in the Eucharistic species and as an act of faith in that selfsame presence. The extended theological introduction sets forth the basic theological truths that must be understood by any Catholic seeking to fulfill the dominical command of "take and eat . . . take and drink."

While the new wider permissions for the distribution of Holy Communion under both kinds should be readily embraced, we should not neglect the indispensable catechesis required for an appreciation of the Church's understanding of the presence of Christ in the Eucharistic species. It is true that "Holy Communion has a more complete form as a sign when it is received under both kinds" (*Norms*, no. 20, citing GIRM, no. 281). But a fruitful reception of the Blessed Sacrament under both species presupposes an understanding of the doctrines of real presence and concomitance, as well as the reasons for the Church's restoration of this ancient practice. Thus, there must be a clear understanding that

> the extension of the faculty for the distribution of Holy Communion under both kinds does not represent a change in the Church's immemorial beliefs concerning the Holy Eucharist. Rather, today the Church finds it salutary to restore a practice,

when appropriate, that for various reasons was not opportune when the Council of Trent was convened in 1545.[11] But with the passing of time, and under the guidance of the Holy Spirit, the reform of the Second Vatican Council has resulted in the restoration of a practice by which the faithful are again able to experience "a fuller sign of the Eucharistic banquet" (ibid.). (*Norms*, no. 21)

4. Participation

The last of the aspects of the Sunday Mass that Pope John Paul II asked us to examine is our notion of participation (see *Dies Domini*, no. 51), with the note that "there is a need too to ensure that all those present, children and adults, take an active interest, by encouraging their involvement at those points where the liturgy suggests and recommends it."[12]

The *General Instruction of the Roman Missal* (GIRM) often speaks of full participation by the faithful as the *motive and goal* for the revision of various parts of the Roman rite. For example, paragraph 5 insists that certain parts of the Eucharistic celebration that have fallen into disuse or neglect should be restored, since these belong to the laity by "virtue of the rank of each within the people of God." The use of the vernacular itself (GIRM, no. 12), the reception of Communion under both kinds (nos. 13-14), the introduction of Masses for various needs and occasions (no. 15), the involvement of the laity in the planning of liturgical celebrations (no. 18), the adaptation of gestures within the rites (no. 24), and the renewed forms specifically of celebrating the penitential rites, the profession of faith, the general intercessions and the Lord's Prayer (no. 36)—all are to be understood as fostering increased participation, demanded by "the nature of the celebration . . . and for the Christian people, [they are] a right and duty they have by reason of their baptism" (GIRM, no. 19). Perhaps nowhere is this theology of participation more dramatically stated than in the passage in the GIRM describing the Eucharistic Prayer: "The meaning of the Prayer is that the entire congregation of the faithful should join itself with Christ in confessing the great deeds of God and in the offering of Sacrifice" (no. 78).

From *Sacrosanctum Concilium* to the present day, we have proclaimed that the goal of the liturgical reform is our full, conscious, and active participation in such a gathering. But what does that really mean? Whether in gathering rites, word, or Eucharist, how do we participate in this gathering which Christ has called to himself?

The first, fundamental, and most essential level of our participation in the Liturgy and in the Church is our participation in Christ's paschal death and rising, on so intimate a level that we become the mysteries we celebrate—we are transformed into the image of him whose body and blood we eat and drink. A full participation in such a mystery means a full donation of myself. A conscious participation in such a mystery means an intentional dying to my own will and a rebirth to God's will for me. An active participation in such mysteries means that I actively let go of everything I have and embrace only the obedient and active love of Christ, who now lives in me.

What is the most important element in good Liturgy and of active participation in it? An embrace of Christ and him crucified. The matter of good Liturgy is not a matter of knowing the right words or putting the furniture in the right place. The matter of good Liturgy is, rather, the conversion of human hearts by participation in the sacrifice of Christ to his Father. As Leo the Great once preached, "What is as priestly as to dedicate a pure conscience to the Lord and to offer the spotless offerings of devotion on the altar of the heart?"[13]

Closing

At the conclusion to *Dies Domini*, the Holy Father Pope John Paul II reminded us that "there is a need for special pastoral attention to the many situations where there is a risk" (*Dies Domini*, no. 80) that the Lord's day may be diminished in the life of the Church.

A careful implementation of the third edition of the *Missale Romanum* is an indispensable ingredient in the restoration of Sunday to its place as a *dies Domini* and a *dies Ecclesiae*. For only when the word is effectively proclaimed and received by open hearts, when the Eucharist is understood as the source and summit of our entire lives, when Christ is recognized and embraced in the sacred species, and when participation in the Liturgy is rooted in the hearts of every member of the gathered assembly—only then will the Church's vision of the Lord's supper on the Lord's day become real.

Reflection Questions

1. Several aspects of our modern culture seem to militate against the Eucharist as a sacrament of unity. How do divisions of language and culture, consumerism, and liberal and conservative labels divide our churches?

2. How can we foster a spirit of active listening and participation in the proclamation of the Word of God at Mass?

3. How can Eucharistic Adoration outside Mass lead followers to a fuller participation in the celebration of the Holy Eucharist?

4. How can an appreciation of the internal and external dimension of participation in the Mass help us to draw closer to Christ?

NOTES

1. John Paul II, Apostolic Letter *On Keeping the Lord's Day Holy* (*Dies Domini*) (1998), no. 46, http://www.vatican.va/holy_father/john_paul_ii/apost_letters/documents/hf_jp-ii_apl_05071998_dies-domini_en.html.
2. *General Instruction of the Roman Missal* (GIRM) (Washington, DC: USCCB, 2004), no. 16; see no. 13.
3. Second Vatican Council, *Dei Verbum* (*Dogmatic Constitution on Divine Revelation*), no. 21, in *Vatican Council II: Volume 1: The Conciliar and Post Conciliar Documents*, edited by Austin Flannery (Northport, NY: Costello Publishing, 1996).
4. John Paul II, Address to the bishops of Washington, Oregon, Idaho, Montana, and Alaska on the occasion of their visit *ad limina apostolorum* (October 9, 1998).
5. *Holy Communion and Worship of the Eucharist Outside Mass* (New York: Catholic Book Publishing, 1976), no. 1.
6. See Second Vatican Council, *Sacrosanctum Concilium* (*Constitution on the Sacred Liturgy*), no. 14, in Flannery.
7. See Paul VI, *Mysterium Fidei* (*The Mystery of Faith*) (1965), http://www.vatican.va/holy_father/paul_vi/encyclicals/documents/hf_p-vi_enc_03091965_mysterium_en.html; *Holy Communion and Worship of the Eucharist Outside Mass*; and John Paul II, *Ecclesia de Eucharistia* (*On the Eucharist*) (Washington, DC: USCCB, 2003).

8. See USCCB Bishops' Committee on the Liturgy, *Thirty-One Questions on Adoration of the Blessed Sacrament* (Washington, DC: USCCB, 2004).
9. Sacred Congregation of Rites, *Eucharisticum Mysterium* (*Instruction on the Worship of the Eucharistic Mystery*) (1967), no. 50, in Flannery.
10. See USCCB, *Norms for the Distribution and Reception of Holy Communion Under Both Kinds for the Dioceses of the United States of America* (Washington, DC: USCCB, 2002).
11. See Council of Trent, Session xxi (July 16, 1562), *De doctrina de communione sub utraque specie et parvulorum* (DS 1725-1734; TCT 739-745).
12. See *Sacrosanctum Concilium*, nos. 14; 26; John Paul II, Apostolic Letter *Vicesimus Quintus Annus* (4 December 1988), 4; 6; 12: AAS 81 (1989), 900-901; 902; 909-910.
13. Leo the Great, Sermo 4:1.

BIOGRAPHICAL NOTE

Msgr. James Patrick Moroney, a priest of the Diocese of Worcester, is executive director of the Secretariat for the Liturgy of the United States Conference of Catholic Bishops. In 1999 he was appointed by Pope John Paul II as one of two English-speaking consultants to the Congregation for Divine Worship and the Discipline of the Sacraments, and he serves on the Vox Clara Committee that advises that same congregation on the translations of the Latin Missal into English. Msgr. Moroney holds a license on sacred theology from the Catholic University of America and has pursued theological and liturgical studies at the Pontifical Gregorian University in Rome and at the Pontifical Liturgy Institute at St. Anselmo's.

CHAPTER 7

The Eight Beatitudes of the Eucharistic Prayer

FR. CHARLES E. MILLER, CM

"I have eagerly desired to eat this Passover with you." —Luke 22:15

A man was smoothing out the concrete on his newly paved driveway when his two children came dashing out of the house. They ran right through the still wet concrete. Their father let out such loud invective that his wife looked out the window and demanded of him, "What's wrong with you? Don't you love your children?" Trying to calm himself, he replied, "Yes, in the abstract but not in the concrete."

Eight Essential Elements

We cannot leave the Eucharistic Prayer in the abstract. It can, and indeed must, be formative of our spirituality. The prayer is composed of eight essential elements. These elements are the eight beatitudes of our liturgical life. They are the summit of all Liturgy, the indispensable source of the true Christian spirit.

Throughout its long and unbroken tradition of celebrating the Mass, the Church has been very careful to maintain the essence of these eight ingredients to form the Eucharistic Prayer: the Preface, the epiklesis, the Institution Narrative (which includes the Consecration), the Anamnesis or Memorial, the Offering or Anaphora, the Intercessions, the Final Doxology, and the Acclamations.

The prayer begins with the Preface, which gives thanks and praise to God the Father for his work of salvation through the life, death, and Resurrection of his Son, or sometimes for a special aspect of that work that corresponds to the day, the feast, or the season. Within the Preface comes the first acclamation, when we join together in the heavenly hymn of praise "Holy, holy, holy." The Preface continues its motif of thanks

---

Adapted from Chapter 7 of Fr. Miller's book *Liturgy for the People: A Trilogy*, volume 2, *The Celebration of the Eucharist* (New York: Alba House, 2001). Used with permission.

and praise until the epiklesis, by which the Church calls upon God the Father to send the Holy Spirit to transform bread and wine into Christ's Body and Blood for the sacrifice. During the Institution Narrative and Consecration (both are one element), we celebrate the very sacrifice that Christ himself instituted at the Last Supper when, under the appearances of bread and wine, he offered his body and blood to the Father, gave them to his apostles to eat and drink, and then commanded them to carry on this mystery in his memory.

We acknowledge this mystery of our faith by one of the four Eucharistic Acclamations.[1] The first proclaims the nature of the mystery: "Christ has died, Christ is risen." The second and fourth express the meaning of the mystery: "Dying you destroyed our death, rising you restored our life," and "Lord, by your cross and resurrection you have set us free." The third, drawn from the eleventh chapter of the First Letter to the Corinthians, describes how we share in the mystery by Communion: "When we eat this bread and drink this cup, we proclaim your death, Lord Jesus, until you come in glory." Then follows the Anamnesis, the memorial in fulfillment of Christ's commandment, whereby the Church lives the memory of his death and Resurrection. Within this context of memorial comes the Oblation or Offering: the Church joins Christ in the offering of himself to the Father as the victim of our sacrifice.

We then return to the epiklesis, this time asking that we who share in the Body and Blood of Christ may be brought together in unity by the Holy Spirit. This petition for unity flows into the Intercessions, which make clear that the Eucharist is celebrated in communion with the entire Church of heaven and earth and that it is offered for all its members, living and deceased. The Final Doxology gives all glory and honor to the Father through, with, and in Christ in the unity of the Holy Spirit. The Acclamation known as the Great Amen expresses our affirmation of the entire Eucharistic Prayer.

The Eucharistic Prayer

The Eucharistic Prayer is the summit of all liturgical prayer. It is the heartbeat of the Church. Within this prayer we find a profound, ecclesial spirituality—a Church spirituality rather than an individualistic one, both the way to pray and the way to live. That is why these elements are like the eight beatitudes from the Sermon on the Mount.

Church Spirituality

First, this prayer illustrates that the foundation of our spirituality is the truth of the Blessed Trinity. This great reality of faith shapes our relationship with God. We pray to the Father through the Son in the unity of the Holy Spirit. Jesus by his death and Resurrection has won for the Father a holy people. He opened his arms on the cross to embrace us in an act of love by which he has drawn us into a union with himself that is so intimate that we have actually become part of him—part of his body, his mystical body, the Church. Liturgical spirituality is not as concerned with looking at the person of Christ as it is with looking in the same direction with him to the Father. Through Christ we have become sons and daughters of God. With Christ we call out to God in prayer and call upon him as *Abba*, Father. Church prayer is family prayer. It is the prayer of God's children; therefore, it is the prayer of those who are brothers and sisters of Christ, and brothers and sisters of each other.

At this point allow me to urge you to pick up your New Testament and turn to the Letter to the Ephesians. Please find the first chapter, verses three through fourteen. The passage has three sections. The first (vv. 3-6) emphasizes God the Father and his relationship to us. The second section (vv. 7-12) focuses on God the Son, who came into the world as our redeemer. The third section (vv. 13-14) highlights the Holy Spirit. The trinitarian relationships presented in these three sections are a beautiful foundation for appreciating the trinitarian orientation of the Eucharistic Prayer. Note that the action of each person on our behalf is in praise of God's glory, a liturgical orientation.

A Living Memory

When children are growing into adulthood they reach a point at which they are fascinated with family history—provided, of course, that their history contains happy memories. When it does, they love to look at photo albums that contain pictures of their parents when they were young and those from when they themselves were children. These photo albums are being replaced these days by home videos and CD-ROMs; but whatever the method may be, to remember is a beautiful thing.

Our Church's family history begins with creation and follows the movement of God through Abraham and all his offspring in what we call the "Old Testament," just as we talk about the time when our parents were young as "the old days." We recall that in the fullness of time God sent his Son to be our Savior, and so our attention is drawn primarily to the eldest son of the family, to Jesus himself. In fact, all the events of "salvation history" come to a focus in the person of the incarnate Son of God, especially in the Paschal Mystery of his death and Resurrection.

The Eucharistic Prayer is "anamnesis," memorial. It is not a photo album or even a video. These devices are only images of people and their actions. Liturgical memorial is reality. By the almighty power of God it makes real what we recall. Liturgical memorial makes present what it memorializes. In the Eucharistic Prayer, after the Institution Narrative and Consecration we profess that in union with Christ we are acting "in memory of his death and resurrection" (Eucharistic Prayer II); that we "celebrate the memory of Christ," God's Son (I); and that we call "to mind the death your Son endured for our salvation [and] his glorious resurrection" (III). We fulfill the command of Jesus: "Do this in memory of me" (I-IV).

The Paschal Mystery

Our spiritual life must embrace a constant meditation and reflection on the life, death, and Resurrection of Christ, the reality that leads to our celebration of the Eucharist and flows from it. The Paschal Mystery is the fulfillment of Christ's coming into our world; it is the center of all liturgical celebration, and it must become the preoccupation of our prayerful thoughts. St. Paul presented the Paschal Mystery succinctly: "[Jesus became] obedient to death, / even death on a cross. / Because of this, God greatly exalted him" (Phil 2:8-9). Mary expressed the Paschal Mystery in her Magnificat: "My spirit rejoices in God my savior. / For he has looked upon his handmaid's lowliness" (Lk 1:47-48). God's lifting up of the lowly is part of the Paschal Mystery.

Liturgical spirituality sees the Paschal Mystery everywhere. When night turns into day, that is the Paschal Mystery. When a seed dies in the earth and rises to become a fruitful vine, that is the Paschal Mystery. When a woman's birth pains are transformed into the joy of giving life to a child, that is the Paschal Mystery. When an alcoholic is recovering from the slavery of addiction and beginning a new life of freedom, that is the Paschal Mystery. When food satisfies hunger and drink quenches thirst, that is the Paschal Mystery. When health overcomes sickness, when love drives out loneliness, when reconciliation produces the fruit of repentance—all of these are the Paschal Mystery. It is no wonder that during the Eucharist we exclaim, "When we eat this bread and drink this cup, we proclaim your death, Lord Jesus, until you come in glory."

The Sacrament of Baptism is our first experience of the Paschal Mystery. We are a people who have been plunged into the death of Christ, and we have been raised with him to newness of life (see Rom 6). Baptism is a one-time experience, but this initial sacramental sharing in the Paschal Mystery leads us to the Eucharistic celebration of the Paschal Mystery that we are privileged to participate in every Sunday—even daily—and that gives meaning and purpose to our lives. Our ultimate sharing in the Paschal Mystery is our physical death, which brings us to enjoy the fruit of the Resurrection, everlasting life. Liturgical spirituality never forgets the Paschal Mystery.

Liturgical Thanksgiving

When we remember, we are motivated to express thanks and praise to God. In fact, that is the expression with which we begin the Eucharistic Prayer, in the Preface. Liturgical spirituality makes us realize that we belong entirely to God and that life is to be a continual act of thanks and praise that we offer through Christ to our loving Father. The sentiments of those prayers that we call Prefaces teach us "to turn to [God] in all our troubles, and give [him] thanks [and praise] in all our joys."[2]

The Offering

The Anamnesis, the memorial of the death and Resurrection of Jesus, is completed by the Oblation, which may be termed the "Offering" or the "Anaphora." "Father," the third Eucharistic Prayer says after the acclamation, "calling to mind the death your Son endured for our salvation, his glorious Resurrection and ascension into heaven, and ready to greet him when he comes again, we *offer* you in thanksgiving this holy and living sacrifice" (my emphasis). We pray again to the Father, "May [Christ] make us an everlasting gift to you." This offering, this giving of ourselves as a gift to the Father, tells us that to live the Paschal Mystery—to make it the foundation of our spirituality—we must do by intention what Christ did by his actions: we must place ourselves completely into the hands of God our Father. To live liturgically is to live for the Father as dutiful and loving children, as Jesus himself did and as he wishes to continue to do through and in us.

The Communion of Saints

Next we pray that "we, who are nourished by his body and blood, may be filled with his Holy Spirit and become one body, one spirit in Christ." This prayer, which is epiklesis, leads to the Intercessions, which reflect and express our unity with the whole body of Christ on earth, in purgatory, and in heaven. It is a great joy to realize we are one family with Mary, the Mother of God, with Joseph her husband, and with all the angels and saints. It is a consolation to believe that we can pray for "those who have died in the peace of Christ and all the dead whose faith is known to [God] alone" (Eucharistic Prayer IV). It is strengthening to know that we are part of the Church, united with brothers and sisters all around the world. The Intercessions remind us that the Catholic faith is not an individualistic religion. The central idea of the Second Vatican Council proclaims this Good News: "It has pleased God, however, to make men [and women] holy and save them not merely as individuals without any mutual bonds, but by making them into a single people, a people which acknowledges Him in truth and serves Him in holiness."[3]

The Trinity

The great Doxology tells that we have indeed learned to pray as Jesus has taught us and that we pray to the Father as one with Christ. It affirms the orientation of prayer: we give all glory and honor to the Father through, with, and in the Son in the unity of the Holy Spirit. God has given us his divine Son incarnate as our intercessor, our mediator, our priest. The Doxology also assures us that life is to be lived as children in God's family, that we are brothers and sisters of one another.

The Doxology concludes this great prayer of thanks and praise and parallels the formula we use to conclude our prayers of petitions: "Through him, with him, in him, in the unity of the Holy Spirit, all glory and honor is yours, almighty Father, for ever and ever."

We employ the Hebrew word "Amen" many times throughout the Mass. When we do so at the conclusion of the Eucharistic Prayer, we call it the "Great Amen" because this prayer is the Great Prayer of our Catholic faith. Sometimes it is said that "Amen" means "So be it," "Yes," "Certainly," or something similar, but that is not true. "Amen" means "Amen." It should not, and really cannot, be translated. We do well, however, to visualize it with an exclamation point: "Amen!" The Great Amen should always be sung. When we reflect on the meaning of prayer, perhaps we can see that the many words which we express to God really all come down to this one word, "Amen!" The liturgical spirituality of the Eucharistic Prayer will be fulfilled when, through our final sharing in the Paschal Mystery, it becomes God the Father's turn to say of our lives, "Amen!"

Reflection Questions

1. What elements of the Eucharistic Prayer are missing from our personal and parish spiritualities? How can we participate more fully in the Eucharistic Prayer and incorporate these elements into our spiritual lives, and how can we help others to do so?

2. The life of the Blessed Trinity is a constant theme in the Eucharistic Prayer. How can we deepen our understandings of the doctrine of the Trinity and join our hearts more effectively to the Eucharistic Prayer?

3. How do elements of the Eucharistic Prayer such as the memorial, Paschal Mystery, and the communion of the saints resonate with contemporary culture? How can we more effectively teach such fundamental elements of the Catholic faith, preparing ourselves and others to celebrate the Eucharist?

Notes

1. There are only three in Latin, and there are variations in other languages.
2. See Roman Missal, Preface II of the Holy Spirit. in the Roman Missal.
3. Second Vatican Council, *Lumen Gentium* (*Dogmatic Constitution on the Church*), no. 9, in *The Documents of Vatican II*, edited by Walter M. Abbott (New York: Guild Press, 1966).

Biographical Note

Fr. Charles E. Miller, CM, a Vincentian Priest, was ordained in 1956. He spent virtually his entire priestly life at St. John's Seminary in the Archdiocese of Los Angeles, where he served as rector from 1978 to 1987 and later as the Von der Ahe Professor of Liturgy and Homiletics. In 1989 Cardinal Mahony presented him with the archdiocesan *Laudatus* award "for excellence in the promotion of the liturgical life of the parishes and people of the Archdiocese of Los Angeles." Fr. Miller passed away in February 2005, one month after he received the Pro Ecclesiae et Pontifice Medal from Pope John Paul II.

CHAPTER 8

Eucharist as Formation for Mission

SR. ANN REHRAUER, OSF

> *[After his baptism by John], Jesus returned to Galilee in the power of the Spirit . . . He came to Nazareth, where he had grown up and went according to his custom into the synagogue on the sabbath day. He stood up to read and was handed a scroll of the prophet Isaiah. He unrolled the scroll and found the passage where it was written: / "The Spirit of the Lord is upon me, / because he has anointed me / to bring glad tidings to the poor. / He has sent me to proclaim liberty to captives / and recovery of sight to the blind, / to let the oppressed go free, / and to proclaim a year acceptable to the Lord." / Rolling up the scroll, he handed it back to the attendant and sat down, and the eyes of all in the synagogue looked intently at him. He said to them, "Today this scripture passage is fulfilled in your hearing." —Luke 4:14, 16-21*

This declaration of Jesus in the fourth chapter of St. Luke's Gospel outlines his mission as well as the mission of the Church and that of every Christian who has passed through the waters of the font and who journeys to the new and eternal Jerusalem:[1] to proclaim liberty, to free the oppressed, to preach the Gospel, to proclaim and inaugurate a year of jubilee. It is, therefore, appropriate that we reflect upon the Eucharist and its ability to form and transform us as we carry out our mission as Christians.

The life of faith begins in Baptism; but it is in the Eucharist, the climax of initiation into the Christian community, that Christian identity and mission are acquired, expressed, and celebrated. For the Eucharist forms and transforms those who celebrate, enables them to love with the mind and heart of Jesus, and sustains them when their vision fades or when the Kingdom itself seems beyond their reach.

While the entire Eucharistic celebration is expressive and formative, each of the principal rites helps us to understand and to focus on the various aspects of the mission to which we are called. The Entrance Rites highlight the communal dimension of our mission: to become the body of Christ—sons and daughters of the one Father, brothers and sisters in Christ, and brothers and sisters to one another. The Liturgy of the Word expresses the dual dimension of personal conversion and evangelization required for mission. In acknowledging Jesus as Lord and Savior, we experience our need for redemption as well as the commission to bring others to know God's great love and mercy. The invitation to join ourselves with the priestly action of Christ in the Liturgy of the Eucharist enables us to offer the acceptable sacrifice of praise and to be joined with Christ in the meal that is a sign of the life to come. And finally, in the Dismissal Rites we are commissioned to live the mystery we have celebrated. Having remembered what Jesus said, we are sent to do what Jesus did.

The Mission to Become Community in Christ

The Eucharistic celebration is, by its nature, expressive and constitutive of community: it expresses the unity that exists among the members, and the very act of celebrating together deepens that unity. The liturgical assembly that Christ gathers for worship is not a cluster of individuals who simply sense a need to be together for support, nor is it a group of like-minded people who happen to be in the same space at the same time praying privately. Rather, the Eucharistic assembly is called together by Christ to pray with one heart and one voice, fashioned by the Spirit to fulfill Jesus' command to "do this" in memory of him—but to do it together.

Pope John Paul II, in his letter on the celebration of Sunday, *Dies Domini*, reminded us that "those who have received the grace of Baptism are not saved as individuals alone, but as members of the Mystical Body, having become part of the People of God."[2] In gathering to celebrate the Eucharist, we come together to make time and space for God and for each other, to tell and to hear the wondrous story of our salvation, to celebrate the dying and the rising of the Lord, and to take and break the bread that is Christ so that we might know and experience him more deeply as we await his coming in glory. We are called to this celebration from various backgrounds and places—no longer individuals, strangers, and aliens, but members of God's household. And if we enter into the dying and the rising of Jesus, the one Lord, one faith, and one Baptism that we share are great enough to overcome any religious, social, or political issues that might divide us.

At the very beginning of the Eucharistic celebration we experience our solidarity and unity. Transitioning from the everyday world to sacred time and space, we enter the church—the house of God and the house of the community—to be greeted by other members who welcome and invite us to enter into the Mystery we have come to celebrate. Icons, vessels and vesture, sights and sounds, ritual movement, and familiar words and actions draw us beyond the limits of this particular time and place. As the Liturgy unfolds we blend our voices in the entrance song, and in the harmony we sense again the richness of belonging to a community. The priest then proclaims that we have gathered in, with, and under the name of the Father, Son, and Holy Spirit. Together then we share the silence, hearing the common and personal call of the penitential rite, understanding our need for redemption, and becoming more aware of God's mercy and power to forgive. As the priest "collects" all our individual prayers, he speaks with one voice and prays in the name of the one people.

Our parishes work hard at welcoming new members—at helping us to learn each other's names and recognize each other so that our spiritual communion can build on the human dimension of community and hospitality. But even in large communities where people may not know each one by name, or sometimes even by sight, we can still worship together because Christ's Spirit makes us one.

Like the citizens of every age, twenty-first–century Americans struggle with the concept and the demands of community. Longing to belong and to be part of something greater than ourselves, we still cling to the rugged individualism and "true grit" that have served us well in times of great adversity in our history. But that very self-reliance and tenacity can militate against the virtues of self-sacrifice, surrender, and peace making needed for the communal activity we call "worship." In communal activity, individual rights and wants must sometimes yield to the common good, in order to enable people to move from an "I" mentality to "we." The Christian community predates us and will exist long after we die. But it is in the midst of this community that we experience the truth: our individual vision and love of God are far too narrow. Only together can we fully know and image the Christ, who is Lord of history and our personal Savior. This knowledge and image come to completion only after our death.

The difficulty of becoming a true community is neither a modern phenomenon nor a characteristically American one. From the earliest days the apostles Paul and James had to remind the Church of that aspect of her mission. And all of us who celebrate realize that our community is imperfect. Racism, economic injustice and exploitation, self-righteousness, religious labels and stereotypes, and even differences about the Liturgy strain and fragment our unity. But if we enter into the mystery of the Eucharist with the mind and heart of Christ, the very act of taking, giving thanks for, breaking, and eating the Bread of Life together has the power to overcome all divisions and to deepen our awareness and experience of our unity in Christ. So while the Church "makes" the Eucharist, at the same time the Eucharist "makes" the Church.

The Call to Conversion and the Mission to Evangelize

The Church and the individual Christian are always *"semper reformanda"*—constantly being called to conversion, to a deeper love of God and neighbor, and to greater fidelity to the Gospel *they* profess. Each time we celebrate the Liturgy of the Word, we tell and hear the marvelous story of our salvation—accounts of our ancestors in faith, saints and sinners, prophets and apostles, holy men and women through whom God's Spirit has kept the promise alive. But the story reaches its climax in the life and death of Jesus, whom God appointed heir of all things, making him the firstborn of many brothers and sisters. And though we tell the stories year after year, each time we gather we hear them in a new way. We never exhaust the meaning or the challenge of the Scriptures.

The proclamation of the word announces the Good News of Christ's victory over sin and death and denounces sin and injustice. And we find in ourselves both kinds of stories: sinners in need of conversion, and the beloved redeemed by the blood of the Lamb. The words of Scripture are not nostalgic reminiscences of those grown older and wiser, nor sagas of our family's roots and wings. Rather, the word of God is life-giving truth that comforts and consoles us in difficulties, encourages and sustains us in frustration as we deal with our own weakness, and teaches us what it means to put on the mind and heart of Jesus. But that same word cuts sharper than a sword when we are complacent or dishonest, when we fail to listen and respond, when we are less than the Body of Christ. Just as the prophet Isaiah preached to Israel, enmeshed in issues of commerce and survival, he accuses us today. While we may not blatantly sell a person for the price of a pair of sandals today, we are consummate consumers on an island of plenty in the midst of a world community of poverty and famine. Daily our brothers and sisters go hungry because of our selfishness or indifference, because of world debt and economic exploitation, because of the control that conglomerates and multinational corporations seem to have over our lives, and because of causes so complex that we can hardly imagine them—all making the struggle for justice and charity overwhelming. And in the midst of this overwhelming reality, the Scripture presents the seemingly simple mandate: "this . . . is the fasting that I wish: / releasing those bound unjustly, / untying the thongs of the yoke"; "Only to do the right and to love goodness, / and to walk humbly with your God"; "whatever you did for one of these least brothers of mine, you did for me."[3]

The word of God confronts us in words we can understand but also with the truth in uncompromising language. While the Scriptures call us to a conversion that is personal and communal, they also call us to share the word. The task of the new evangelization is the endeavor not of religious professionals, but of all who profess to know and love the Lord. "Go therefore and make disciples" is the mission of all of us who bear the name of Christ Jesus.

Transformation for Mission: From Death into Life

The Eucharist is always a communal action because it is the action of the Church that gathers and joins itself to the action of Jesus Christ. Each celebration of the Eucharist makes present for us the self-offering of Jesus and enables us to be active participants in Jesus' response to what the Father has done in him for the salvation of the world. For those of us who come to offer our lives, our hearts, and our hands with Christ in the Eucharist, transformation is certain. In the saga of Abraham and the sacrifice of Isaac, divine intervention stayed the hand of the angel of death. But in the life of Jesus, God did not spare his own Son from death, but rather sustained him and enabled him to give his life as a ransom for us. And the Father will do the same for us. God does not promise to rescue us from the difficulties of life, but he does promise to love and sustain us and never abandon us.

For Christ and for Christians, transformation is achieved only through pain and suffering. Day follows night and Resurrection comes only after death. Celebrating the Eucharist is about entering into the death and the surrender of the Lord, being willing to be broken and shared in the everyday tasks of life, as he was broken and shared. Speaking of the laity particularly, the Second Vatican Council taught in *Lumen Gentium*:

> for all their works, prayers and apostolic undertakings, family and married life, daily work, relaxation of mind and body, if they are accomplished in the Spirit—indeed even the hardships of life if patiently borne—all these become spiritual sacrifices acceptable to God through Jesus Christ (cf. 1 Pt 2:5). In the celebration of the Eucharist these may most fittingly be offered to the Father along with the body of the Lord. And so, worshipping everywhere by their holy actions, the laity consecrate the world itself to God. (no. 34)

Sent Forth on Mission

The purpose of the Liturgy is not to escape life but to return us to our everyday tasks refreshed and renewed for the journey. In the long run, the Christian's mission is all about the journey. It is not by accident that John's Gospel lacks an institution narrative and instead provides the account of Jesus' washing the feet of his disciples on the night before he died. While the homilist tries to break open the word and to help us make the connection between the Scriptures and our lives, it is our task to do the final translation. Theologians, poets, and novelists have tried to depict the Last Judgment as a means to illuminate the context and meaning of a life of faith. Chapter 25 of St. Matthew's Gospel issues the very clear and uncompromising verdict: you either did or did not feed the hungry, clothe the naked, give drink to the thirsty, visit those in prison, or bury the dead.

From the earliest days of the Church, there was the realization that true faith and true worship demands that we practice justice. Justin Martyr described the Sunday gathering in the early Church: "those of us who have resources come to the aid of all who are in need and we are always assisting one another."[4] In our lifetimes, the pioneers of liturgical reform, such as Lambert Beaudin and Minnesota's Virgil Michael, saw in the Church's Liturgy the impetus and potential for transforming society into the City of God. If there is a dichotomy between our worship and our life, we have not worshiped well.

If we truly encounter Christ in the Liturgy, we will be different after the celebration. But for many of us who celebrate regularly, we experience so little transformation at times and so little passion to transform society. The celebration becomes routine, or perhaps we do not listen with our hearts as well as our ears. At times we are caught up in other things and find it hard to enter into the Liturgy. But then come those graced moments when we recognize God's justice (which is very different from human perceptions) as the word is proclaimed and broken open in the homily. The parable of the workers who were hired at different times but were all paid the same wage offers lessons about Kingdom justice that have nothing to do with "earning" but rather with the graciousness of God who gives all as gift. We sing the refrain that in Christ there is neither Jew nor Greek, neither slave nor free, no longer male nor female (Gal 3:25). We hear more clearly the words of the Eucharistic Prayer or a Communion antiphon and sense the connection with our lives. The first requisite for doing justice is recognizing injustice—not only in our society, but in ourselves. The second aspect that makes the mission so difficult is that, in opposing the social forces that exploit or perpetrate evil, we may not use the means of violence or disrespect that we want to change. Only by understanding the meaning of Christ's redemptive suffering can we continue to work for justice without becoming the very things we abhor. Third, in the midst of unjust systems, when we seem very small and inconsequential, the example and the presence of Jesus helps us to continue the task of proclaiming and building the Kingdom that has been entrusted to us.

In the sacrifice of the Mass, Christ's Body given for us and his Blood poured out for the forgiveness of sins are offered to God for the salvation of the world. In Eucharist, Christ is present and is offered as "the sacrifice which has made our peace"[5] with God in order that "we may be brought together in unity" by his Holy Spirit.[6] Each time we gather, we come to worship—which means the focus is on God rather than on ourselves. It is a celebration that is communal—far more challenging than private prayer. In this celebration we are asked to make space for others (in the pew and in our lives), to surrender to the rhythm of the ritual, to offer praise and thanks, to acknowledge that we are creatures who stand before God, and finally to enter into the dying and rising of Christ in order to be open to the transformation he offers.

Each time we celebrate the Eucharist, we are a changed community. And each time we enter into the mystery of the dying and the rising of the Lord, we do so with different levels of faith and devotion. Each time we come to offer our praise and thanks, we bring other parts of our lives to offer with Christ to the Father. And hopefully, each time we come, we surrender more of our will and become more open to the Father's will for us.

Reflection Questions

1. The desire to belong to a community of others is deeply rooted in every human person. Is your local church community centered on Christ or on the individuals' needs and desires? How does it reflect the splendid variety of the human family? How does your gathering reinforce artificial barriers?

2. How does your participation in the Mass compel you to proclaim the Good News of our salvation to all the world? Do you receive the strength to always speak the truth? Does your participation cause you to act justly and to seek out those whom the world has forgotten or thrown away?

3. How is your experience of Christ's dying and rising in the Holy Eucharist rooted in the sacrifice of your daily life? How can your daily living out of the Paschal Mystery find inspiration in participation in the Mass?

Notes

1. See Second Vatican Council, *Lumen Gentium* (*Dogmatic Constitution on the Church*), nos. 33 and 34, in *Vatican Council II: Volume 1: The Conciliar and Post Conciliar Documents*, edited by Austin Flannery (Northport, NY: Costello Publishing, 1996).
2. John Paul II, Apostolic Letter *On Keeping the Lord's Day Holy* (*Dies Domini*) (1998), no. 31, http://www.vatican.va/holy_father/john_paul_ii/apost_letters/documents/hf_jp-ii_apl_05071998_dies-domini_en.html.
3. Is 58:6, Mi 6:8, and Mt 25:40, respectively.
4. Cited in Lucien Deiss (ed.), *Springtime of the Liturgy: Liturgical Texts of the First Four Centuries*, translated by M. J. O'Connell (Collegeville, MN: The Liturgical Press, 1979), 3.
5. Eucharistic Prayer III.
6. Eucharistic Prayer II.

Biographical Note

Sr. Ann Rehrauer, a Franciscan sister from Green Bay, Wisconsin, currently serves as president of the Sisters of St. Francis of the Holy Cross. Previously, she was an associate director of the Secretariat for the Liturgy of the United States Conference of Catholic Bishops from 1995 to 2000. A liturgist and a canon lawyer who specializes in liturgical law, Sr. Rehrauer has been a teacher, a diocesan liturgical consultant, and chancellor of the Diocese of Green Bay.

CHAPTER 9

Eucharist and Justice

SR. JOYCE ANN ZIMMERMAN, CPPS

O f the ten decades making up the last century of the second millennium, perhaps the 1960s can be most compellingly connected to a reflection on the relationship of Eucharist and justice.[1] In the 1960s—with, for example, the Beatles and Elvis—music came to be more than a collection of simply pleasing sounds. Suddenly the physical involvement of the musicians played an important part: long hair, gyrating hips, outlandish costumes were as much a part of the music as the notes themselves. Devotees not only sang the music but grew hair and wiggled and dressed like the music makers. Participation had been brought to a new level. The screaming and swooning of the fans were but symbols of this participation.

It was also during the 1960s that war, the Vietnam War, was first brought into people's living rooms, complete with body counts and pictures of blood and gore. Suddenly the practical horrors of war couldn't be relegated to someplace "out there" or "over there" but instead became a part of everyday lives. Some parents actually saw their bloodied and killed children right in front of them, as their comfortable living room television sets beamed body-strewn battlefields. Participation had again been brought to a new level. The anti-war demonstrations indelibly printed on imaginations were but symbols of this participation.

And finally, it was during the 1960s that the Second Vatican Council was announced, convened, and closed. The nightly newscasts reported the speeches and interventions, right alongside the rock stars and war reports, and transmitted pictures of the long lines of prelates gathered for an event that would change the Church forever. Suddenly, church affairs were made public and talked about—not just by the hierarchy, but by the official observers (admitted to a Council and including women, both unprecedented events), and not from news reports but from the people of God who actually saw and heard the events live. Participation had been brought to a new level. *Sacrosanctum Concilium's* (*Constitution on the Sacred Liturgy*) call for "full, conscious, and active participation" was but a symbol of this participation.

These three vignettes show how participation reached new levels, with new implications. In the past, people had participated in the Liturgy, but in a different way. Their participation was from the "outside": the priest said Mass, and the congregation comprised unnecessary onlookers. Mass meted out graces and contributed to the holiness of countless millions of Catholics throughout the ages. But Mass was Mass; what people "took away" from it was a list of moral platitudes, generally learned in the sermon, and religious devotional practices that were more or less faithfully carried out throughout their everyday living.

Vatican II changed all that, at least in principle. Mass no longer "belongs to Father." It is now the celebration in which the assembly gives praise and thanks to God as it unites itself with the sacrificing Christ, entering into his dying and rising Paschal Mystery. And this makes all the difference in the world—because we now *participate* in the Eucharistic rite, we can no longer leave the sacred spaces of worship and go on our way. We leave *transformed*. We are different. And because we are different, our lives can never be the same.

These two notions—transformation and new selves involved in everyday living—guide the remainder of these reflections. My position is not that Eucharist "compels" us to do justice, as something apart from Mass. Rather, we do justice because the Eucharist transforms us into just persons.

A Note on Justice

All too many of us think too quickly of "social justice" when the word "justice" comes up. Certainly social justice needs everyone's active involvement, and some people are uniquely gifted and called to minister full-time in this important way. But not everyone is an Oscar Romero or a Blessed Mother Teresa. We must take care not to think that the relationship of Eucharist and justice applies only occasionally to all of us (when, for example, we are moved to write a letter to a government representative) or that it applies primarily to those engaged in these special ministries. Justice has a broader venue: all of us are called to live justly.

To be sure, justice is social by its very nature. Both biblically[2] and theologically,[3] "justice" refers to right relationships; justice is the standard for living in community and establishing relationships among its members. One concern throughout the Bible, but especially in the Old Testament, is that all people must have their basic needs fulfilled, among them land, food, clothing, and shelter.[4] This is one reason for why justice often concerns the rights of the poor. The notion of justice, however, goes beyond this to include living rightly in all aspects of life. Further, justice involves not only right relationships within the human community, but our right relationship with God. Closely associated with this is the notion of "righteousness": we are considered just or righteous when we are both in right relationship with God and with each other.

One recurring theme—especially in the psalms and prophetic literature—is that one cannot worship (be in right relationship with God) unless one is in right relationship with members of the community.[5] One reason is that God is creator and sovereign of the world; everything that is comes from God. We offer God worship because God is Creator and because God has called a people to be God's own. Worship is our response to all that God has done for us, acknowledging God's greatness and our being created. At the same time, worship demands of us a respect for God's creation and God's people. To put it another way, we cannot worship God in a vacuum. Our relationship with God necessarily implicates our relationship with each other because Creator and created are inseparable. This is one connection between worship and justice.

Another way to get at this relationship is to reflect on the familiar Gospel parable about places at table (Lk 14:7-14). Jesus is dining in the house of a leader of the Pharisees and notices how the guests choose places of honor. One approach to the parable is simply from a human perspective of social standing and face saving. It is embarrassing to take a place of honor and then be asked to move; it is pleasing to sit at a lower place and then be asked to move to a place of honor. The parable might also be interpreted at a deeper level. The clue comes when, after telling the parable, Jesus instructs a host to "invite the poor, the crippled, the lame, the blind" (Lk 14:13). Rather than inviting a guest because he or she can repay the host in kind, Jesus admonishes, hosts should invite those who cannot repay themselves, for the hosts will be repaid by God "at the resurrection of the righteous" (Lk 14:14). This special meal is named "messianic" when it includes those who have less than we have; the meal becomes the occasion to share equally in God's gifts of the land so that everyone might share in the abundance of God's blessings. By choosing a lower place at table, we align ourselves with the poor and needy; we acknowledge our relationship to God as creature to Creator. In a sense this choice is the profoundest act of worship, for we witness by our action to a right relationship to God through our relationship with others. Further, being one with the poor means that we have firsthand knowledge of their plight and are better able to meet their needs, to serve them.

It is most telling that Chapter 14 from Luke's Gospel concludes with Jesus' making rather harsh remarks about the cost of discipleship: "If anyone comes to me without hating his father and mother, wife and children, brothers and sisters, and even his own life, he cannot be my disciple" (Lk 14:26). Jesus concludes, "In the same way, everyone of you who does not renounce all his possessions cannot be my disciple" (Lk 14:33). Giving up all possessions makes us all equally dependent upon God. It transposes our focus from our own needs and pleasures, with our limited vision and restricted relationships, to an enduring perspective derived from our most basic relationship to God: creature to Creator. His statement is not literally about the negatives of hating and giving up; it is about right perspective and right relationship. Everything we possess as humans pales in comparison to a single-hearted relationship with God and the gift and blessings that brings. This is the basis for our human relationships with each other.

Let's be practical. This interpretation of the parable and of justice doesn't require us to give up asking our friends over for dinner. It does invite us to reflect on our own means—great or modest—and how much we share with others. This isn't a matter of putting money in a poor box. The Scriptures remind us that justice entails *acting* on behalf of others so that right relationships are well established. Moreover, as St. Thomas Aquinas reminds us, justice is a virtue or a habit. This means that serving others through meeting their needs—whether physical, spiritual, emotional, or psychological—is a *way of life* for us. Acting justly isn't something we do once in a while when a special opportunity comes our way—it is a habitual way of relating. When we reach out to those near us, we establish good habits that help us see no real difference between doing for our immediate family, doing for our neighbor down the street, or doing for someone half a world away. All of our doing, then, emulates God's pervasive care for all of God's creation.

The Eucharist That Transforms

The foregoing remarks on justice have been developed so far from the viewpoint of ourselves as creatures relating to our Creator. When we turn attention to Eucharist, we come at justice from a different direction: from that of God, and of how Eucharist itself transforms us into creatures who share in the divine and are thus called to act like the Divine.

Celebration of Eucharist, ideally, brings about a transformation in the worshipers. The proclamation of God's word always challenges us to a greater surrender in order to take up our baptismal commitment to live the dying and rising mystery of Christ. The Eucharistic Prayer draws us into our Christian story. By hearing God's mighty deeds on our behalf—and especially Jesus' salvific life and ministry—we are encouraged, invited, and enabled to participate ritually in redemption. This participation is perhaps best symbolized by Communion, whereby we eat *and become* sharers in the divine life, the divine I AM. The transformation is not only of identity—we become more deeply members of the body of Christ—but also one of perspective. Because we become God-like, we also assume God's perspective. Here is perhaps the deepest meaning of our creation in the image of God: we take on God's perspective, his way of being and acting, so we can be and act the same. It is also the deepest meaning of Eucharistic transformation: by being transformed more perfectly into the body of Christ we are transformed into *being just persons*, as God is just (see Chapter 14 of John's Gospel, where Jesus speaks of the intimate relationship between him and his Father and also between him and us).

Since God always has concern for the "widow, orphan, and sojourner"—a biblical formulary for anyone without means, family ties, land, or, in short, anyone in need—when we take on God's perspective through Eucharistic transformation, God's concerns become our concerns. Identifying with and serving the poor is God-like behavior consistent with our gradual transformation into being a Eucharistic people. To share in Eucharist without a concomitant concern for others is to eat and drink to our own condemnation (see 1 Cor 11:17-34).

New Selves Living Justly

Being human means being born into the community of humanity. Being Christian means being born into the dying and rising of Christ. Birth itself initiates lives turned to justice because being born means to be in relationship. The wonderful gift of Eucharist is that Jesus Christ continues to give himself to us as food and drink that transform us into the presence of the Risen Christ for others. Thus armed with God's perspective on creation and creature, we are better able to reach out to the widow, orphan, and sojourner.

The relationship of Eucharist and justice is reciprocal. Eucharistic transformation offers the perspective needed to look upon all others as sisters and brothers in creation and in Christ. When we are so related, choosing what is right and good for another is "natural." Doing justice—caring for the other, especially those in need—opens us to the kind of self-surrender essential for Eucharistic action to be transformative. Eucharist transforms us for the sake of others; doing for others is "practice" in the self-surrender that makes this transformation possible.

The just living of transformed, new selves focuses on the other rather than self. This is the "dying to self" demanded by commitment to the cross. It is the self-emptying that makes space for God's divine life to blossom within us. It may happen in the great things done by the Oscar Romeros and Blessed Mother Teresas; the world is a much better place for committed people like these. But as wonderful as these actions on behalf of justice for others are, they are not enough. Eucharist and justice require that each one of us—whatever our daily circumstances—live as true disciples, reaching out to the leper, healing the sick, feeding the hungry, teaching the unlearned, setting free those trapped with myriads of demons, preaching to the spiritually hungry. And yes, it means raising those who are dead to new life.

Reflection Questions

1. How might you participate in Eucharistic celebrations so that you are truly transformed more perfectly into the risen presence of Christ for others, living with God's perspective?

2. With God's perspective, how do you view those around you—at home, work, leisure, parish, the poor and disadvantaged of the world? How do you respond to them?

3. If "justice" means right relationships with God, self, and others, how do you cultivate this habit in your daily living? What needs to be changed in your life? What gives you hope? Courage?

NOTES

1. For further background on my thinking on this topic over the past years, see my *Liturgy as Living Faith: A Liturgical Spirituality* (Scranton, PA: University of Scranton Press, 1993) and "Eucharist and Reconciliation: A Jubilee Year Gift," *Liturgical Ministry* 9 (Winter 2000): 19-27.

2. For a very fine summary of the biblical notion of justice, see Camilla Burns, "Biblical Righteousness and Justice," *Liturgical Ministry* 7 (Fall 1998): 153-161.

3. Thomas Aquinas includes justice among the principal (moral) virtues and defines it as a habit in which members of a community render to each other his or her due by a constant and perpetual will (see Pt. II-II, Q. 58, Art. 1).

4. In this regard, it is interesting to see what was the concern during the fiftieth year, the jubilee year. See Lev 25:1-55, which spells out the basic requirements for the jubilee year. For an excellent commentary, see J. Frank Henderson, "Justice and the Jubilee Year," *Liturgical Ministry* 7 (Fall 1998): 190-195. That entire Fall 1998 issue of *Liturgical Ministry* was devoted to the theme Liturgy and justice; ample bibliography appears in the notes for each article and would make excellent further reading.

5. See, for example, Ps 9, 72, 113, 140, 146; Mic 6:8; Amos 8:4-6; Jer 22:15-16; Is 58:6-7.

BIOGRAPHICAL NOTE

Joyce Ann Zimmerman, CPPS, is a Sister of the Precious Blood of Dayton, Ohio. She is the director of the Institute for Liturgical Ministry in Dayton, founding editor of *Liturgical Ministry*, a past advisor to the Bishops' Committee on the Liturgy, an adjunct professor of Liturgy, and a liturgical consultant. She holds a pontifical doctorate in theology from St. Paul University, Ottawa, Ontario, and a PhD from the University of Ottawa.

CHAPTER 10

Adoration of
the Blessed Sacrament

FR. JEREMY DRISCOLL, OSB

It is not possible to love Christ without adoring him. Indeed, one of the greatest joys of our loving him is to adore him. Of course, we love him in other ways also: by keeping his commandments, by our loving one another, by sharing with him in prayer the joys and sorrows of each day. If there are many ways of loving him, there are also different ways of adoring. One of the privileged ways is to adore him in the Blessed Sacrament. But what does this mean? How is it done? What are we actually doing when we come in prayer before the Blessed Sacrament in the tabernacle, or when the Sacrament is exposed to our view for veneration? These reflections give some answers to such questions.

It is important to find the right starting point for an answer, and in this regard the Tradition and teaching of the Church are completely clear. Adoration of Christ in the Blessed Sacrament is always to be understood as deriving from the presence of Christ in the actual celebration of the Eucharist; adoration is meant to bring us again to the celebration of the Eucharist with greater fervor and understanding. So adoration begins in the celebration of Mass itself. However, adoration in the Mass is primarily directed to God the Father. It is adoration "in Spirit and truth" (Jn 4:23)—that is, adoration of the Father through Christ, the Truth, and in the Holy Spirit. Nonetheless, in different moments in the course of the Eucharistic celebration, Christ himself is adored in the very elements of the Sacrament: that is, in the bread and the wine that have been transformed into his Body and Blood. The celebration of the Eucharist, the Mass, is an unfathomable mystery. It is the Church's greatest treasure, indeed, her essence. The Eucharist is an inexhaustible fountain, yielding in every generation and in the heart of every believer ever-fresh knowledge of God—Father, Son, and Holy Spirit. Often, however, the actual celebration seems to pass by too quickly, even when we have managed to participate with attention and understanding. So I suggest here that adoration of Christ in the Blessed Sacrament outside of Mass can be best conceived as a meditative contemplation of what is too difficult to grasp and digest all at once during Mass. In prayer before the Blessed Sacrament, I can continue, in quiet reflection, my communion with Christ from Mass, and I can prepare for the next communion. A little history and some theological reflection illuminate why I suggest viewing adoration of Christ in the Blessed Sacrament in this way.

Historical Notes

Adoration of the Blessed Sacrament outside of Mass is a practice peculiar to the Latin church, and it developed only in the second millennium. Such a fact requires some caution and raises questions. We should be cautious, for example, about thinking that such adoration is a practice to be required of all. In fact, this gift is found in some parts of the Church and is given to some to practice, while others are blessed with other gifts and different ways of prayer. Naturally, concerning a practice that was virtually not present in the Church's first thousand years, we will want to explore how it came about.

Reservation of the Blessed Sacrament outside of Mass seems to have been a part of the Church's Eucharistic practice almost from the beginning. But reservation is different from adoration. In the patristic era, the purpose of reservation was so that the sick and others who could not attend the actual celebration of the Eucharist would also be able to communicate.[1] In the second century Justin Martyr told of deacons carrying the Sacrament directly from the Sunday Eucharist to those who could not attend. Towards the end of the same century Tertullian mentioned the faithful carrying the Sacrament from the Eucharistic celebration so that they could communicate later in their homes. In the early third century, *The Apostolic Tradition,* a church order that described various liturgical practices, included the same custom, as well as that of taking special care of the particles of the Eucharist.

When I say that this custom is to be distinguished from adoration, I simply mean that the purpose of reserving the Eucharist was not so that Christians could come before it in prayerful adoration. The purpose was rather that they might receive it. But these very early practices of the Church show at least two essential aspects about the Eucharist that we want to retain for our own understanding of prayer before the Sacrament. First, the ancient practices show that reservation is done primarily with a view toward receiving the Sacrament. It comes from the actual celebration and extends that celebration to those who cannot be present at it. The scope of Eucharistic *reservation* is so that people might *receive* the Eucharist. A second aspect shown in the ancient practices is an implicit, instinctive understanding that the presence of Christ perdures in the consecrated bread beyond the time of the actual celebration. The practice of actually adoring Christ present in the bread developed slowly as a logical unfolding of this implicit understanding.

In drawing attention to these practices, I am speaking not about the heart of the Eucharistic celebration but rather about something deriving from it. The heart of the celebration, from the patristic era to the present, has always been what the name "Eucharist" means: thanksgiving. Thanksgiving for our salvation is offered to God the Father through Jesus, his Son, in the Holy Spirit. To speak of thanking the Father "through Christ" is not a throwaway phrase. The Church's thanks to the Father could never be worthy of the divine majesty, were her gifts of bread and wine not transformed into the body and blood of Christ offered for the world's salvation on Calvary. This pouring out of the life of Jesus for the sake of the world was his act of adoration of the Father; this is what the Church likewise holds up in thanksgiving to the Father. This is why the Eucharist is called a memorial of the Lord's death, and the very same is our thanksgiving to the Father. This memorial is thanking him "through Christ," adoring him through Christ: "Through him, with him, in him, in the unity of the Holy Spirit, all glory and honor is yours, Almighty Father, for ever and ever."

So in the heart of the Eucharistic celebration, it is primarily the Father, not Christ, to whom worship is directed. Yet this does not say it all, for from the beginning there has also been a sense of Christ himself being hymned and adored in the community's gathering for prayer.[2] The Council of Nicea in AD 325 faced only one specific question about Christ: was Christ to be considered a creature, however highly exalted, or was he to be considered as divine, existing from all eternity? The latter was deemed to express the apostolic faith of the Church. Such clarity about the divinity of Christ was useful for the Christian community, even if it raised other problems;[3] and it inevitably influenced how Christians understood their Eucharistic experience. A sense of the presence of the crucified and now glorified Christ had always pervaded the community assembled to give thanks to the Father through him. Now, with the language of Nicea, the community could understand that the Christ who was present and active in the Eucharistic assembly was no less than "God from God, Light from Light, true God from true God." Inevitably—and quite rightly—liturgical practice expanded to include gestures and words appropriate to this belief: namely, an adoration also of Christ through whom the Father is adored.

If we further consider what the patristic Church understood about the bread and wine of the Eucharistic rite, we see at that time an almost instinctive sense of the nature of a sacrament. The bread and wine were a *sacrament* of the Lord's body and blood.[4] That is, by means of bread and wine we come into contact with something that now would otherwise be beyond reach: namely, the risen and glorified body of Christ, no longer confined to space and time. So by means of a sacrament, we come into contact in space and time with that which transcends space and time. The sacrament is a middle term between us and the transcendent body of the Lord. I can touch and hold another person in my hands, make contact with another through touch. It is not quite the same with Christ, though it is *like* this. With Christ I touch the *sacrament* of his body and thereby make contact with his body through my body. The sacramental experience is at one and the same time concrete and transcendent, just as Christ is concrete and transcendent.

The delicacy and precision of this kind of thinking was in part lost in the Latin West during the early Middle Ages. In the ninth century, complicated controversies about how to understand the presence of Christ in the Eucharist swung between two poles. Was Christ to be understood as being truly present (*in veritate*) or only symbolically present (*in figura*)? These poles could not have been considered opposites in the patristic Church, where symbolic presence—presence by means of a sacrament—was not a less real presence, but one appropriate to both the transcendent and concrete reality of Christ. Now, in these controversies, a symbolic presence seemed to mean a less real, a less concrete presence. The alternatives hardened into extreme positions: on the one hand describing the presence of Christ in crudely realistic terms, and on the other describing it as a presence not belonging to the physical world but to something entirely symbolic and spiritual. Neither alternative is correct, though each carries a partial truth. It took several centuries to establish the view that the Eucharist can be real without being crudely realistic, and symbolic without being unreal.[5]

From this context, adoration of the Blessed Sacrament outside of Mass seems to have arisen. First evidence of it appeared in the late twelfth or early thirteenth centuries. A fruit of the controversies was—despite all the wrangling—a stronger sense of the intense presence of Christ in the Eucharist, a sense of wonder in the manner of his presence. From this arose an even greater desire to adore Christ so present—to contemplate the mystery, to gaze on it with awe.[6]

Theological Reflections

With this relevant history thus summarized, a few theological reflections can move beyond the controversies to consider the value of Eucharistic adoration in our own time. Most important is that adoration be linked to the actual celebration of the Eucharist and to the reception of Communion. This has always been at the heart of the reason for reservation and at the heart of the practice of adoration, even if this focus was sometimes lost in the midst of controversies. In our own times the Church has reiterated this teaching with clarity: "When the faithful honor Christ present in the sacrament, they should remember that this presence is derived from the sacrifice and is directed toward sacramental and spiritual communion."[7]

Where the Blessed Sacrament is present, either in a tabernacle or exposed on the altar for adoration, this presence gives evidence that a community has celebrated the Eucharist, with all that this means and implies. We can never adequately grasp how much is accomplished in the community every time the Eucharist is celebrated. We are seeking to understand this more and to contemplate it in a continued adoration of Christ in the sacrament. When I am present before Christ in the tabernacle, it is a time of intimate communion with him simply because I am concentrated on him. I can deepen in a very personal way the communion with him that I have experienced in the communal celebration, a communion which, as suggested in the beginning, is perhaps too difficult to grasp and digest all at once during Mass. The Sacrament exposed on the altar concentrates my attention on the very place where the community has celebrated the memorial of the Lord's death. Generally, the exposition of the Blessed Sacrament is done for the sake of a more communal adoration. Even if I am in silent prayer alone, I am alongside others who adore with me. We adore because we have celebrated. Our adoration increases not only communion with Christ but with one another, expressing one same faith together.

Whether it takes the form of private prayer before the tabernacle or of communal prayer before the Sacrament exposed, the adoration of Christ during the course of the Mass can indicate a proper and fruitful approach to these devotions. It remains true and must not be forgotten, as we have said, that in the Mass it is primarily the Father who is adored, through Christ and in the Holy Spirit. But at moments in the celebration, the ritual act is an act of adoration directed to Christ. Already in the Liturgy of the Word, apart from the general sense of the presence of the risen Lord "who opens our minds to the understanding of the Scriptures" thus causing "our hearts burning [within us]" (Lk 24:32), we have heard prayers like "Lord, have mercy; Christ, have mercy," or "Praise to you, Lord Jesus Christ," together with all the signs of respect and joy that greet the reading of the Gospel. All these are ways in which I can also pray before the Blessed Sacrament.

Nonetheless, it is especially the Eucharistic Prayer and Holy Communion that indicate the sense of adoration outside of Mass. After the priest has pronounced the words of Christ over the bread, he holds it up for our view so that we may seek somehow to penetrate the mystery of its transformation into the body of Christ. Then he genuflects in adoration before it, as all in the community follow his gesture in their hearts and with gestures of their own. He does the same with the cup of wine. Exposition of the Blessed Sacrament is like a freezing of this moment for our continued contemplation. Prayer before the tabernacle is much the same. Such contemplation will help one in the next celebration to be present to the moment with even greater awe and love.

Again, just before Communion the priest holds up the body of Christ for the view of all, proclaiming, "Behold the Lamb of God!" Already in the Liturgies of patristic times this was a strong moment of adoration of Christ present in the Sacrament. Likewise, one approaches Communion knowing that "I am not worthy" but trusting in his mercy. And just before receiving Communion each communicant is to render a sign of reverence before the Sacrament. Above all, in the reception of Communion, we adore Christ. It is the fundamental attitude with which we receive him. Either in the silent prayer of the whole community that follows immediately or in that silent prayer extended later before the Blessed Sacrament, we can hear his words echoing within: "Behold, I stand at the door and knock. If anyone hears my voice and opens the door, I will enter his house and dine with him, and he with me" (Rev 3:20). But there is more. For through this wondrous intimacy with Christ, we are taken by him to know another: namely, his Father. Knowledge of Christ becomes knowledge of the Father: "Just as the living Father sent me and I have life because of the Father, so also the one who feeds on me will have life because of me" (Jn 6:57).

I want to hold myself before this mystery. I want to penetrate it more and more. I want Jesus' words to be fulfilled in me and in the whole Church: "On that day you will realize that I am in my Father and you are in me and I in you" (Jn 14:20). I cannot love Christ without adoring him. Love of him promises me trinitarian communion and eternal life: "Whoever loves me will keep my word, and my Father will love him, and we will come to him and make our dwelling with him" (Jn 14:23).

Reflection Questions

1. Fr. Driscoll suggests that "it is not possible to love Christ without adoring him." How is this love actualized and strengthened in time spent in prayer before the Blessed Sacrament?

2. How do the origins of Eucharistic reservation explain the relationship between Eucharistic adoration outside Mass and our participation in the celebration of the Mass? How can this relationship be strengthened?

3. How is the communal dimension of the celebration of the Eucharist always present in Eucharistic adoration? How can an appreciation of this communal dimension be strengthened?

Notes

1. "Patristic era" refers to the Church of the first five or six centuries after the period of the composition of the New Testament. The earliest witnesses for this question are Justin Martyr, *Apology* I, 65-67; Tertullian, *On Prayer*, 19; *The Apostolic Tradition of Hippolytus*, nos. 36-38; Cyprian of Carthage, *On the Lapsed*, no. 25. What follows is to be found in these texts.
2. This is a long and complex story, for there was a kind of tension in pre-serving a clear and coherent monotheism while at the same time adoring both the one whom Christ called God and Father and Christ himself. For more on this, see Larry W. Hurtado, *One God, One Lord: Early Christian Devotion and Ancient Jewish Monotheism* (Philadelphia: Fortress Press, 1988).

3. For example, if Christ is God and the one whom he calls Father is God, how many gods are there? Any answer other than "one God" was impossible, and yet Christ and the Father are not the same thing, so how many gods are there? Subsequent councils will be needed in order to give solid answers to these questions.

4. Other terms were also used: *figure* of his body and blood, *type* of, *image* of, *mystery* of, and so on. For examples, see Tertullian, *Against Marcion*, 4: 40; Ambrose, *On the Sacraments*, 4: 5; Augustine, *Exposition on the Psalms*, Psalm 3:1.

5. I have summarized here very briefly complex theological questions that stretch over three or four centuries. An immense literature studies all this. Two useful summaries would be the following: Enrico Mazza, *The Celebration of the Eucharist: The Origin of the Rite and the Development of Its Interpretation*, translated by Matthew J. O'Connell (Collegeville, MN: The Liturgical Press, 1999), 161-224; Nathan Mitchell, *Cult and Controversy: The Worship of the Eucharist Outside Mass* (New York: Pueblo, 1982), 66-195.

6. This is the best fruit of the controversies, a fruit that shows itself in deep Eucharistic devotion in the lives of many saints through the subsequent centuries. See E. Longpre, "Eucharistie et experience mystique" in *Dictionnaire de spiritualite* IV/2, 1590-1621. There could also be a polemic edge to various practices of adoration: e.g., against those who claim the presence is "merely symbolic," one asserts realism by adoring the very bread and wine. This held true later also in response to the position of some Protestant Reformers, who believed in either a soft symbolic presence or in the idea that the presence of Christ in the bread and wine does not outlast the actual celebration. Being on one's knees before the tabernacle or the exposed Sacrament obviously expresses a different faith.

7. *Holy Communion and Worship of the Eucharist Outside Mass* (New York: Catholic Book Publishing, 1976), no. 80.

BIOGRAPHICAL NOTE

Fr. Driscoll is a Benedictine monk at Mount Angel Abbey in Oregon and a senior fellow of the St. Paul Center for Biblical Theology. He has an STD in patristic theology and teaches both at Mount Angel Seminary and at the Pontificio Ateneo S. Anselmo in Rome. In 2004, he was named a member of the Pontifical Academy of Theology and also a member of the Vox Clara Committee of the Congregation for Divine Worship and the Discipline of the Sacraments. He was a contributor to the USCCB's *The Voice of the Church: A Forum on Liturgical Translation*.

CHAPTER 11

The Eucharist and Inculturation

SR. DORIS MARY TUREK, SSND

Amassive multiethnic, multicultural program to celebrate the Jubilee Year was taking place at the Los Angeles Convention Center in July 2000. Momentum grew as the events of each day unfolded. Prayer spaces reflected the saints of devotion of many ethnic groups residing in the country. Keynote and workshop speakers motivated participants, who traced their roots to more than 160 countries. Foods representing several countries were enjoyed, and rhythms of other lands evoked clapping and smiles and swaying in time to the beat. At a penance service, those present asked pardon for social sins committed against members of certain racial groups.

It was at the closing Liturgy, however, that the true unity of the gathering manifested itself. As Catholics stood elbow to elbow with other Catholics of many ethnic groups, as songs were sung in some languages and readings proclaimed in others, the oneness of those assembled was palpable. For one bishop, the culmination came at the Our Father, which was recited together by participants, each in their own native tongue. "I truly experienced Pentecost at that moment," he reflected after the Liturgy.

Celebration of the Eucharist in pluricultural communities is not about native dress, nor traditional musical rhythms, nor the sights, sounds, and color creating the perfect photo op. Eucharist in these communities is about prayer: where participation of all of the people is united and directed to the God of all, prayer in a house in which all feel welcome.

A Multicultural Church

The Church in the United States of America is visibly a multicultural Church. Recent census data confirm that our country is already made up of people from many countries, and the immigration continues. The newcomers in an already diverse environment come into a culturally diverse society. The Church has sought to provide welcome and support to immigrants, migrants, refugees and people on the move.[1] They all bring to worship their rich faith lives and traditional religious practices.

Bishops, priests, and lay leaders in every diocese throughout the United States are reaching out to welcome and integrate newly arrived immigrants, making efforts to provide those traditional devotions that many of the newcomers have practiced in their native countries. Experiencing these devotional practices in the United States helps to integrate Catholics from the many ethnic communities into their local parish community and promotes the teaching of communion, conversion, and solidarity that John Paul II advocated his post-synodal exhortation *Ecclesia in America*.[2]

Inculturation and the Liturgy

Liturgy is prayer. It is communal worship. The primary purpose of multicultural liturgical celebrations is to ensure that all present, despite differences in language, culture, socioeconomic status, and level of education, might feel the hospitality of the assembly and the invitation to participate actively in the Liturgy.

Certainly, meeting the multiple linguistic needs of the faithful is essential. The proclamation of the Scriptures is central to the Christian tradition of Liturgy, as are the prayer texts such as Eucharistic Prayers and Collects. No one should be excluded from an understanding of the Liturgy just because they do not understand the language used.

But the churches in our country are not just multilingual; they are also multicultural. Liturgical reform—as mandated by the Fathers of the Second Vatican Council, calling for the "full, active, conscious" participation of those gathered for the Liturgy—has given rise to inculturation in the liturgical celebrations in this country. In the *Constitution on the Sacred Liturgy*, the Second Vatican Council noted that the Church "does respect and foster the qualities and talents of the various races and nations. Anything in these peoples' way of life which is not indissolubly bound up with superstition and error she studies with sympathy, and, if possible, preserves intact. She sometimes even admits such things into the liturgy itself, provided they harmonize with its true and authentic spirit."[3] And as *Varietates Legitimae*, the fourth instruction on inculturation and the Liturgy, states, "As particular Churches . . . deepen their understanding of the liturgical heritage they have received from the Roman Church which gave them birth, they will be able in turn to find in their own cultural heritage appropriate forms, which can be integrated into the Roman Rite where this is judged useful and necessary."[4]

The result has been involvement of people of many different cultural groups in Liturgy planning, as well as a greater participation of members of these groups in Sunday and weekday Liturgies. A few simple principles should be kept in mind when preparing for celebration of the Eucharist in multicultural settings:

- Any attempt at liturgical inculturation must take into account the people, assembled in Christ's name, who often represent diverse cultures, socioeconomic groups, and ages. *Each cultural group has something precious to share* with every other group. It is to the extent that we can share these gifts with one another—without suspicion, fear, or desire for control and dominance—that our multicultural Liturgies will truly be a work of the people. However, before we can authentically participate in multicultural liturgical celebrations, we must first understand our own cultures and devotional customs.

- All who come to Liturgy should feel welcome in God's house. Therefore, a *ministry of hospitality* is vital, so that those who enter the church building are greeted by someone who speaks words of welcome.

- *Preaching* should also be truly multicultural. While the homily should be given in the language of the largest number of those present, preaching in the other languages of those gathered is an important part of acknowledging and respecting the cultures that are represented.

- *Nonverbal communication* is most important. Movement (such as in processions), silence, and the use of symbols can all help to foster unity. Music has the power to gather people together in prayer and praise that words alone do not. The environment and art employed in the worship space, as well as the organization of the interior space of the church building and the design of devotional areas, should all be inviting to the multicultural assembly.

Cultural groups that have a lively devotional life, largely drawn from popular religious practice, offer an invitation to creativity, since the need for devotional images must be in some way respected. As the *Directory on Popular Piety and the Liturgy* observes, "Popular piety is a sign that the faith is spreading its roots into the heart of a people in such a way that it reaches into daily life. Popular religiosity is the first and fundamental mode of 'inculturation' of the faith. While it must always take its lead and direction from the liturgy, it in turn enriches the faith by involving the heart."[5]

More Radical Forms of Inculturation

Authentic inculturation of ritual, then, requires time, patience, and careful preparation. A vast number and array of popular religious practices exist. Some can be integrated into the Liturgy, but others should more properly remain private devotional practices. How can we determine which might best be included in liturgical celebrations?

The *Constitution on the Sacred Liturgy* (no. 23) says that to prepare an inculturation of the Liturgy, episcopal conferences should call upon people who are competent both in the liturgical tradition of the Roman rite and in the appreciation of local cultural values. This includes historical, anthropological, exegetical, and theological competencies. But these competencies should be examined in the light of the pastoral experience of the local clergy, taking into account the advice of wise people of the country, whose human wisdom is enriched by the light of the Gospel. Liturgical inculturation should try to satisfy the needs of traditional culture as well as those affected by an urban and industrial culture.

Conclusion

In *Vicesimus Quintus Annus*, the apostolic letter on the twenty-fifth anniversary of the Second Vatican Council's *Constitution on the Sacred Liturgy*, Pope John Paul II called for a "certain degree of adaptation to the assembly and to individuals, with the possibility of openness to the traditions and cultures of different peoples." Elsewhere in that letter he continued, "A satisfactory development in this area cannot but be the fruit of a progressive maturing in faith, one which encompasses spiritual discernment, theological lucidity, a sense of the universal Church, acting in broad harmony."[6]

Liturgy is the public prayer of the Church. Our sincere efforts to make our Liturgies experiences of prayer for all who come to worship will lead to the formation of truly Eucharistic communities. May Our Lady, Mother of all of the peoples who make up the Church in the United States, accompany us on our journey.

Reflection Questions

1. What implications does the multicultural nature of the Church in the United States have for the way the Mass is celebrated each Sunday? What are some positive and negative ways to take advantage of this opportunity to grow in Christ?

2. Is a multicultural Church characterized primarily by differences in language, or what more significant cultural differences transcend language? In your parish, what cultural differences divide various ethnic groups, and how are these differences experienced by your parish as a whole? How can the pastor and his staff help all parish groups to experience the Eucharist as the sacrament of unity?

3. What are some differences between the adaptation of the Liturgy that is called for at each parish Mass and the more profound adaptation accomplished by conferences of bishops for particular ethnic groups? What kinds of adaptation are envisioned by the Church for your parish Church?

NOTES

1. See Ruth Doyle, *Ministering Together for Immigrants, Refugees, Migrants, and People on the Move at the Beginning of the Third Millennium* (New York: Fordham University, 2002).

2. See John Paul II, *The Church in America* (*Ecclesia in America*) (Washington, DC: USCCB, 1999).

3. Second Vatican Council, *Sacrosanctum Concilium* (*Constitution on the Sacred Liturgy*), no. 37, in *Vatican Council II: Volume 1: The Conciliar and Post Conciliar Documents*, edited by Austin Flannery (Northport, NY: Costello Publishing, 1996).

4. Congregation for Divine Worship and the Discipline of the Sacraments, *Fourth Instruction on the Roman Liturgy and Inculturation* (*Varietates Legitimae*), no. 33, in *Liturgiam Authenticam: Fifth Instruction on Vernacular Translation of the Roman Liturgy* (Washington, DC: USCCB, 2001).

5. In 2001, the Congregation for Divine Worship and the Discipline of the Sacraments issued its *Directory on Popular Piety and the Liturgy: Principles and Guidelines*, which may be helpful in this regard. The directory can be found online at http://www.vatican.va/roman_curia/congregations/ccdds/documents/rc_con_ccdds_doc_20020513_vers-direttorio_en.html.

6. John Paul II, *On the Twenty-Fifth Anniversary of the Promulgation of the Conciliar Constitution* Sacrosanctum Concilium *on the Sacred Liturgy* (*Vicesimus Quintus Annus*), no. 16, http://www.vatican.va/holy_father/john_paul_ii/apost_letters/documents/hf_jp-ii_apl_04121988_vicesimus-quintus-annus_en.html.

Biographical Note

Sr. Turek is staff advisor on multicultural Liturgy for the Secretariat for the Liturgy at the United States Conference of Catholic Bishops. She holds a master's degree in education from Arcadia University and a civil law degree from the Beasley School of Law of Temple University. She also serves as an adjunct professor at The Catholic University of America and the Washington Theological Union. Sr. Turek is a member of the National Hispanic Institute for Liturgy, of the Pennsylvania, New Jersey, and Philadelphia Bar Associations, and of the American Bar Association.